HOMELAND INSECURITY

...AMERICAN CHILDREN AT RISK

Michael R. Petit

With a foreword by Joel J. Alpert, M.D., and Stephen Berman, M.D.,
past presidents of the American Academy of Pediatrics

Published by Every Child Matters Education Fund

www.everychildmatters.org

ISBN 978-0-9790866-0-1

Manufactured in the United States of America
First Edition

Designed by Mary Cherveny

For Mem and Pep

Acknowledgments

Does everybody need so much help when writing a book? I received a lot of it. I am especially indebted to several people. Justin Haas, research associate at Every Child Matters, spent months relentlessly locating and organizing most of the data used in the book. His perseverance was remarkable. Jane Berger, a journalist and writer, also conducted much research and provided invaluable advice on organizing information. She edited several drafts of the book. Mary Cherveny, the book's graphic designer, brought an unusually sensitive eye to the project, giving strong visual appeal to difficult material. I am particularly grateful to my wife, Pamela Day, who listened patiently for a year to my constant ruminations about the book, whether on trains, planes, drives, or walks on the beach. Her advice and support were essential.

All of the staff at Every Child Matters helped with their comments on the book's early draft. Ursula Ellis provided final copy edits. Mario Morino, a terrific friend of children, contributed financial support. Many other friends and colleagues provided encouragement for doing the book.

While I am solely responsible for all of the opinions and interpretation of material presented in this book, much of my thinking was shaped by my lifetime relationship with a wonderful extended family. It also has been influenced by the many ordinary and extraordinary children and families encountered in a working life that has taken me to all the states of this great nation.

HOMELAND INSECURITY
...AMERICAN CHILDREN AT RISK

FOREWORD

As pediatricians and educators, we know that the great majority of young people move through childhood in good health. And like most pediatricians, we've learned that the life chances of children, whether they have health problems or not, are vastly improved when they are the top priority of concerned and supportive families and communities. This support, when combined with our expanded scientific knowledge about healthy human growth and development, and our ability to both prevent and treat illness, assures that the great majority of children sail into young adulthood physically and emotionally healthy, becoming productive members of society.

But this happy story ignores millions of American children, children who are in serious trouble, challenged by problems that should not exist in the world's wealthiest nation. The societal conditions which produce these problems, conditions that we know how to overcome, are the focus of Homeland Insecurity...American Children at Risk by Michael Petit. Homeland Insecurity is a thoughtful, if stinging, analysis of conservative policies and budgets, which Petit argues have failed to address the social and health needs of children. Based largely on U.S. Bureau of Census data and other official sources, Petit's analysis is refreshingly simple, straight forward and clear. It is must reading for political leaders—and for parents and grandparents.

Michael Petit in Homeland Insecurity argues convincingly that the secret to the nation's true wealth, and its competitive advantage, has long been its unparalleled ability to create opportunities for nearly all of its children and families. A combination of public and private sector investments, largely financed through federal taxes, created a vast middle class, both educated and prosperous, which Petit shows has been threatened by the anti-tax/anti-government policies at the heart of conservative ideology, policies which have been dominant for 25 years.

Petit compares the well-being of children in the United States to those in the other rich democracies—the children in the United States are consistently last on key indicators. He compares the well-being of children from state to state and finds wide variation in the data—children fare much better if they happen to live in some states instead of others. Further, and what is likely to spark the greatest discussion, Petit directly challenges the wisdom of conservative ideology by showing that children do much better overall if they live in so-called blue states, where there are higher levels of taxation and investments in children, than if they live in red states, where both taxes and social investments historically and now are less.

Homeland Insecurity includes chart after chart supporting Petit's thesis that anti-tax/anti-government ideology places children at greater risk, whether for low birth weight, infant mortality, premature death, child abuse, no health insurance, incarceration or, most devastating, poverty. The data are convincing and alarming.

Petit reminds us that earlier generations committed the resources needed to lift millions from poverty and to provide better health care, accomplishments that are often forgotten in the heated polarization of today's national politics. These earlier investments led to programs such as Social Security, unemployment and disability insurance, Medicare, and Medicaid providing our nation's most vulnerable with a safety net.

Petit's call to action includes making major new federal investments in children to stop child abuse, insure every child, and much more, calling for $500 billion of the nation's still vast resources to be spent on closing the investment gap in child well-being. Clearly there is nothing magic about these numbers or the time frame, but it is a place to start. At this, the early start of the 2008 election cycle, all of us concerned with children and youth should challenge anyone seeking elected office, especially the presidency, to tell us how they will help children.

Our emotional attachment to children, because they represent our nation's future, is the real power of Petit's message. In the most basic terms, using clear and powerful data, Homeland Insecurity challenges us to make the children and grandchildren we all love our national political priority. Protection, opportunity, health, family and community—these are the elements that make for secure children. As Petit says, "we can do this."

Joel J. Alpert, MD
Professor and Chairman Emeritus, Boston University School of Medicine
Past-President of the American Academy of Pediatrics

Stephen Berman, MD, FAAP
Professor of Pediatrics, University of Colorado School of Medicine
Past-President of the American Academy of Pediatrics

Millions of American children are without health insurance, millions are reported abused and neglected, millions are left unsupervised everyday after school, and millions have parents in a prison system that is crushing families.

1. WE CAN DO BETTER THAN THIS

Since 2001, more than 20,000 American children have paid the ultimate price in a homeland that was anything but secure for them: they were murdered on their neighborhood streets, killed in their own homes, or took their own lives.

Child Deaths 2001-2005

Chart 1.1*[1]

	Child Homicides	Child Suicides	Child Abuse & Neglect Deaths	Total
2001	1,809	1,027	1,321	4,157
2002	1,815	974	1,390	4,179
2003	1,753	918	1,177	3,848
2004	1,792	973	1,383	4,148
2005	1,792	973	1,317	4,082
Total:	**8,961**	**4,865**	**6,588**	**20,414**

* Numbers in italics in table are estimates created by averaging the numbers from previous years

The deaths of these children apparently went unnoticed judging by the near-total silence about them from the conservatives who have dominated the administration and, until recently, controlled Congress.

It goes beyond unofficial government neglect. Under the guise of an anti-government/ anti-tax ideology labeled "compassionate conservatism," the nation has taken a giant step backwards since 2001 in the protection of children and the creation of opportunities for them. Overshadowed by wars, political and corporate corruption, and the dismal aftermath of Hurricane Katrina, what's gone unnoticed were the unrelenting budget attacks by conservatives on social programs that help millions of children.

I didn't plan to write a book. I've written it because, in 37 years as a social worker, I've never seen politicians as unwilling to extend a caring hand to children as those who, until recently, have dominated our national government. They hide behind a narrow definition of family values and profess to care about children, while they vote against the very programs that benefit them. This ideology does not reflect the basic decency I have encountered across the United States among people of all political persuasions, people who want their own children and grandchildren and other people's children and grandchildren to succeed.

Drawing from my own experiences and from mostly official federal data, this book shows that our nation's families face immense obstacles in raising their children and that they can no longer look to their national government for help. It dispels two principal myths upon which conservative ideology is based: first, that government itself—not poverty, lack of opportunity, racism, unemployment, ignorance, or disease—is the enemy; and second, that taxes are evil. These twin misrepresentations mask the fact that generations of Americans, through their democratically elected federal representatives, chose to make social investments— paid for by progressive taxes—which successfully lifted millions into the middle class. The data in this book show that the children harmed most by this ideology live primarily in the South, where politicians have embraced it most enthusiastically. And it shows that major new federal investments in children and families are essential for our future security and prosperity.

Proven health and social programs for children first came under serious attack after the Reagan

Administration took office in 1981. Those still seething from Roosevelt's New Deal nearly 50 years earlier had finally established a toehold in official Washington. Emboldened by the adoption of California's Proposition 13 in 1979, which required approval by 67 percent of voters before local taxes could be enacted, the Reagan Administration now slashed billions from social programs to finance federal tax cuts. The conservatives who controlled the government in recent years expanded this earlier attack.

Except for the modest gains of the Earned Income Tax Credit and the Comprehensive Health Insurance Program adopted during the Clinton years, federal programs have failed to keep pace with the growing needs of children. Federal spending on the elderly has grown much faster, so that about $8.40 is now spent per senior for every federal dollar spent per child.[2] The results are predictable. As seen in Chart 1.2, the elderly poverty rate has plunged thanks to federal programs, mostly engineered by moderates and liberals. Meanwhile, thanks in large part to the erosion of real federal spending on children and families, mostly engineered by conservatives, the child poverty rate is rising again even as the stock market has climbed. Further, more people are uninsured, real wages are declining, prisons are overflowing, and millions of children live in distressed families facing their struggles alone, thanks in large measure to conservative policy.

Lest anyone be misled, the conservative attack on federal spending for children is strictly ideological. It has nothing to do with a purported conservative goal of exercising fiscal restraint: far from it. We've gone from massive federal budget surpluses just six years ago to massive budget deficits today. Part of it is the result of fighting wars, but mostly it's due to revenue-busting tax breaks, poor Congressional oversight on hurricane relief, inflated spending on homeland security and on drugs for the elderly, and rocketing private budget "earmarks" for the likes of Alaska's proposed "Bridge to Nowhere."

Poverty and wealth

Chart 1.2[3]

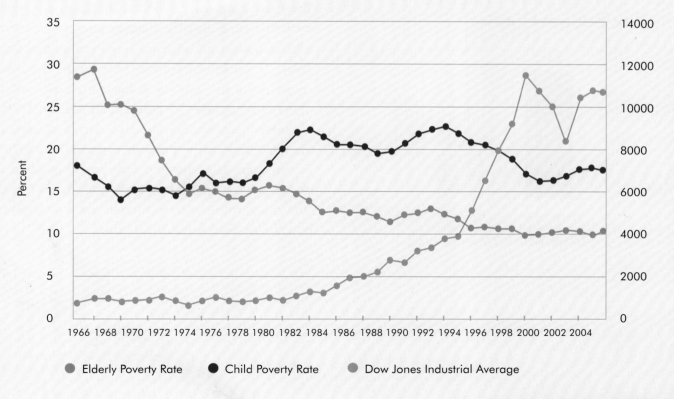

Legend: Elderly Poverty Rate · Child Poverty Rate · Dow Jones Industrial Average

Inevitably, the fiscal recklessness of conservative policy drastically changed federal spending priorities. The health and social needs of children have been completely pushed aside by the sharp elbows of powerful special interests. This failure to spend on children is morally indefensible. It makes our economy less competitive, weakens our ability to shore up an aging population, and saddles our grandchildren with staggering debt. People understand this. That's why poll after poll (Chart 1.3) shows broad public support for new investments in children instead of additional tax breaks. Imprisonment, child abuse, poverty, lack of health care—these conditions exist in America on a scale unknown in the other rich democracies. How have they escaped this fate? They recognize that in modern society we are obliged to rely on each other, and that smart government investments which pull all children forward benefit everyone. Compassionate conservatism isn't helpful. It's a snappy slogan cooked up in the heat of a presidential campaign. Can it serve as a substitute for traditional federal spending on children as its proponents proclaim?

It can't. Because compassionate conservatism is a contradiction in terms. Compassion is generous. The New Testament extends it freely to prisoners, prostitutes, and the poor. It does not say compassion is to be doled out conservatively, in small amounts. The American Heritage Dictionary defines conservative as "tending to favor the preservation of the existing order."[5] It defines compassion as "the deep feeling of sharing the suffering of another in the inclination to give aid or support, or mercy."[6] Compassion is something that can't be found in administration budget and tax policies that favor "the haves and the have mores," as the president boastfully called his political base.

We can do much better than this.

Child Investments Preferred to Tax/Budget Cuts

Chart 1.3[4]

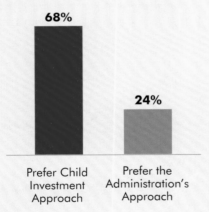

68% Prefer Child Investment Approach

24% Prefer the Administration's Approach

How Did Conservative Voters React When They Learned a Politician's Position on Children's Issues was "Cut! Cut! Cut!"

Texas Congressional District #17 is held today by a Democrat. That's right, the President's Crawford Ranch is represented in Congress by a moderate, one who was targeted for defeat in one of the "DeLay Five" redistricting schemes back in 2004. The incumbent was widely predicted to lose this super red state with its new three-to-one Republican voter advantage. The other four incumbents in the "DeLay Five" races did lose. Not surprisingly, President Bush won his district by 37 points. But to nearly everyone's surprise, the incumbent won his congressional district by four points. Why? Because his opponent, while in the Texas legislature, cut health insurance for 167,000 children and 17,000 pregnant women. Once these facts were publicized, large numbers of Republican and Independent women crossed party lines when they voted. A post-election poll found that 87% of the district's voters believed that government has a moral responsibility to invest in the health, education, and safety of children.[7] Conclusion? Voters of all stripes want children looked after, and extremist views about taxes and the role of government do not extend very deeply into the electorate.

What were distressed children to do when the conservatives who have been running the government refused to extend a helping hand? The implied answer: choose parents who are not in prison, who are not mentally ill or drug addicted, who are not abusive, uninsured, uneducated or low-wage earners.

President Bush and former majority leader powerhouse Tom DeLay hold up Texas as their vision of what America would look like if they had their way. But is that really what Americans want? Is it even what Texans want? Texas ranks 33rd in per capita income, yet in many indicators of child well-being it ranks at or near the bottom. For example, with 24.6% of its children uninsured, Texas has the highest rate of uninsured children in the country.[9] And in one recent year, child abuse deaths in Texas totaled 212, twice as many as in the next highest state.[10]

8

In the following chapters, official U.S. statistics are presented which document the social and economic problems of hard-working families and their children. They also are presented in comparison to the other rich democracies, the Group of Seven, better known as the G7.* Other statistics spotlight conditions in Texas—the home of compassionate conservatism—so we can see how well children have done there. Other charts show the well-being of children in "red" states (those which voted Republican in the 2004 presidential election) versus "blue" states (which voted Democratic) as an indication of state support for the key elements of the Republican or Democratic party platforms. These charts confirm that differences in political philosophies do make a difference for children.

Of the book's seven chapters, four address specific issues facing children and families—health, child abuse, imprisonment, and poverty. There are many other equally important issues, such as housing, education, and racism which need to be addressed as well, but they are not addressed directly in this book. Excellent references on many issues faced by children and families can be found at **www.everychildmatters.org.**

* Omitted from that comparison is the newest member—Russia—of what is now the G8, since few observers actually believe Russia is one of the world's eight richest democracies.

Overall Child Well-being Rank
Top States vs. Bottom States • Chart 1.4[11]

Rank	State
1	New Hampshire
2	Vermont
3	Connecticut
4	Minnesota
5	Iowa
6	Utah
7	New Jersey
8	Nebraska
9	North Dakota
10	Massachusetts
41	North Carolina
42	Kentucky
43	Alabama
44	Georgia
45	Arkansas
46	Tennessee
47	South Carolina
48	New Mexico
49	Louisiana
50	Mississippi

This chart shows that the majority of states ranked in the top 10 for child well-being are blue. They generally tax themselves at higher rates and make more investments in programs serving children. The bottom-ranking states, all of them red, generally favor lower taxes and much lower state spending on social programs. There are 17 charts in this book comparing the well-being of children among the states. The charts show that 77% of the states in the top ten are blue and 23% are red. They show that 91% of the bottom ten states are red and 9% are blue. Not all the blue states show good numbers on child well-being outcomes, nor are all the red states' numbers bad. It's clear, however, that the anti-government/ anti-tax policy approach predominant among the red states has not worked for many children. A new policy approach, relying more on public investments, is necessary to produce better outcomes in the health, education, and protection of children.

At the time this book went to press, the mid-term election in November 2006 moved control of the Congress from mostly conservative domination to what is likely to be mostly moderate to liberal control. Whether the new policies they propose will tilt more in the direction of new investments in children remains to be seen.

2. HEALTHY CHILDREN
IF IT'S GOOD ENOUGH FOR CONGRESS...

Things seemed to be going well enough for the young family of five—mom, dad, and three kids—until the four-year-old was diagnosed with a debilitating disease. They moved in with her parents and mom quit her job to care for the child. Dad continued his full-time job as a car detailer and took a part-time job as a convenience store clerk to pay for the child's medical care—$16,000 a year. The family had insurance, but it didn't cover sick children with a pre-existing condition. Dad earns too much to qualify for government assistance. They are not optimistic about the future.

Among the world's rich democracies, this case, and hundreds of thousands like it, could only occur in one of them, the richest one—the United States.

That's because the other rich democracies have national health insurance and we don't. Actually, that's not exactly true. Some lucky Americans do have the equivalent of national health insurance: the 535 members of Congress and their families. They don't worry about the cost of the best health care for their families because taxpayers pay most of it for them. That leads me to wonder: if inexpensive, high quality, comprehensive, taxpayer-subsidized health insurance is good for Congress, then why isn't it good for the rest of us?

Uninsured children are four times as likely to delay medical care and twice as likely to go without eyeglasses or medicines.[1] Some will lose their hearing because a preventable infection was not treated. Many will not be immunized against easily preventable communicable diseases. Simple health problems will become major ones.

Despite superb high-tech medical treatment that is recognized worldwide, the American health insurance system is so full of holes that we rank last among the rich democracies on the two most important health measures—infant mortality and longevity.

There are about nine million children at any moment without health insurance.[2] Almost all of them have at least one working parent. Over a two-year period, some 27 million children will be without coverage for at least some time.[3]

How the U.S. Compares to the Other Rich Democracies

Chart 2.1[4]

Infant Mortality Rate 2004, per 1000 Live Births	G7 Countries	Life Expectancy at Birth in years, 2004
3	Japan	82.5
4	Germany	79
4	France	79.5
4	Italy	81
5	United Kingdom	78.5
5	Canada	80.5
6	United States	77.5

The U.S. infant mortality rate is 20 percent higher than Canada's and the United Kingdom's, and 100 percent higher than Japan's. As for life expectancy, Canadians live about 1000 days longer than Americans, the Japanese almost 2000.

Our present health insurance system is a mess:

- Families are forced to send both parents to work because it may be the only way to get insurance. The mother in one young family I know works full-time just to get coverage. Her husband's small business can't afford insurance. Her entire salary is eaten up by child care for their toddler and infant twins.

- Families make decisions on jobs, move to different locations, decide to get married or not, based on health insurance considerations.

- Thousands of families with special-needs children have surrendered legal custody of them to state governments because it is the only way to get the health services they need.

The pediatrician explained that her seven-year-old patient needed braces, but the request was rejected by the insurance company. Not good, I thought, but lots of other kids don't have perfectly straight teeth either. No, no, she said, not that kind of braces—LEG braces. Her patient had a degenerative disease and the insurance company said it couldn't justify the expense in view of the child's short life expectancy.

It doesn't have to be this way. For more than 100 years, the federal government has provided the principal leadership for improving the health of the nation's children. In 1900, the infant mortality rate was 162 deaths per 1,000 live births[5]—today it is six, a drop of more than 90 percent.[6] Maternal mortality rates at birth plummeted almost 99 percent over the same period.[7]

These and other remarkable improvements are the result of decisions by earlier generations to tax themselves for the benefit of their grandchildren and great-grandchildren. Federal standards were adopted for safe drinking water, sewage treatment, and the pasteurization of milk. Social welfare programs extended nutrition and health care services to the poor. Federal bureaucracies were established to support health research and to stop the terror of widespread communicable diseases. Spectacular successes in public health, under the leadership of the federal government, produced great gains in the health of average Americans.

Serious problems remain:

The U.S. birth rate for females 15-19 is double that of the next highest G7 country, the United Kingdom, and 12 times higher than Japan's.

Chart 2.2[8]

G7 Countries	Annual births per 1000 females 15-19 (2000-05)
Japan	4
Italy	6
France	9
Germany	11
Canada	19
United Kingdom	24
United States	49

- 900,000 children—nearly one out of every five two-year-olds—have not been immunized against the main childhood diseases, even though every $1 spent on vaccinations saves $16 in treatment costs.[9]

- The infant mortality rate in 2002 increased for the first time in more than 40 years.[10] The U.S. rate is just slightly better than Cuba's and is 27th among rich democracies.[11] The black infant mortality rate in Washington, DC is worse than that of 55 countries, including Libya.[12]

- The United States ranks 30th in maternal mortality at 14 deaths per 100,000 live births.[13] The rate among U.S. black women is four times that of whites.[14]

- The United States is the only rich democracy that does not guarantee prenatal care for all pregnant women.[15]

- Despite major declines in the overall U.S. childhood death rate, the United States ranks 33rd in death rates for children under age five, a rate more than double Japan's, and half again that in France, Germany, and Italy.[16]

- In 2003, 2,018 children and teens died from gunfire.[17]

- Six million children and youth have a serious emotional disturbance—as many as 80% do not receive appropriate services.[18]

- Nearly three million children have learning disabilities, over one million have speech or language problems, more than half a million are mentally retarded, about five-hundred thousand children have autism disorders, some seventy-two thousand have serious hearing loss, and about fifty-five thousand children are legally blind.[19]

- More than six million American children live with at least one parent who is dependent on alcohol or an illicit drug.[20]

- Nearly 400,000 children under five have elevated lead levels in their blood.[21]

G7 Health Insurance Coverage

Chart 2.3 [22]

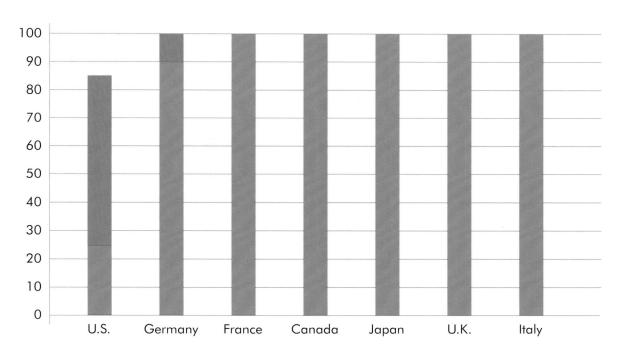

■ Percent of Population Solely Covered by Private Insurance

■ Percent of Population Eligible for Public Health Care Coverage (2002)

Virtually everyone has health insurance in the rest of the G7 nations. In the United States, 46.6 million—8.3 million of them children—have no insurance, and millions more are inadequately insured. Infant mortality rates are lower and longevity rates are higher in the other countries than in the United States—and their per capita spending for health care is much lower.

Millions of U.S. children have no health insurance at all or inadequate insurance. Why don't the other rich democracies have the same kind of insurance problems that we do? We spend $5,267 per capita on medical care, nearly two and one-half times the median spent in the other rich democracies.[23] How do they produce better health outcomes at far lower costs? The answer is pretty simple, as seen in Chart 2.3 above. They treat access to health care, and therefore medical insurance as a public good from which everyone benefits. Because they declare everybody eligible for health care through a government-run, single-payer system, Canada's entire healthcare system holds administrative costs to 16.7 percent of total health expenditures.[24] In the United States, those costs constitute a staggering 31 percent of total health expenditures. There is not a single government agency that wastes anything near 30 percent on administrative costs. After all, it's not as if the U.S. government can't administer large programs efficiently: the giant Social Security Administration has administrative costs of less than one percent.[25]

A review of billing requirements in comparable Canadian and U.S. hospitals is revealing. A handful of people in the billing department of a Toronto hospital spend most of their time sending bills to Americans who crossed the border for medical care. In a Boston hospital, a staff of 352 spends all of its time establishing eligibility and documenting every pill and Band-Aid to satisfy the onerous billing demands of private insurance companies.[26]

Because Canada benefits from the efficiencies of a single-payer system where everybody is covered from birth to death, there are no prohibitions on pre-existing conditions, and there's no need to screen people out, to require co-payments or spend-downs, or to bill people for insurance premiums or for services received. In Canada, personal bankruptcy because of medical expenses is simply unheard of.

Even corporate giants are brought to their knees under our hopelessly inefficient system. One reason General Motors has faced possible bankruptcy is because of the uncontrollable costs incurred by the company to insure more than a million workers and retirees. These costs are higher than the steel that goes into every Chevrolet, and they are costs that foreign competitors do not face because their countries have national health insurance.

The inefficiency of the status quo might be justified if it could deliver services effectively, but it can't. So why don't we have a single payer system in the United States? Why is it that conservative U.S. politicians vilify the Canadian and British systems even though the citizens of these two countries express wide support for their national health services?

Because at the end of the day these same politicians derive benefits in the form of campaign contributions from a medical care system driven by the bottom line interests of profit-making hospitals, drug companies, nursing home chains, private medical practices, and, especially, the medical insurance industry. These for-profit entities are thriving not because of their efficiencies— after all, we have the most wasteful and expensive system in the world. Rather U.S. medical spending, approaching $2 trillion annually, is so enormous and so profitable that the industry adamantly opposes any serious initiative that comes before Congress to change things.[27] In the last nine elections, campaign contributions from the medical industry totaled $620 million.[28] Until the financial relationship between the industry and its friends in Congress is broken, the medical industry corporate giants will always succeed in blocking change.

What possible justification can there be for the existence of nearly 1,300 U.S. health insurance companies— each with a CEO, shareholders, receptionists, sales people, and claims processing departments?[29] A 2004 study by Harvard's Medical School reported that the medical care bureaucracy costs the United States nearly $300 billion a year. It estimated that national health insurance would save at least $286 billion per year on paperwork![30] That's enough to insure every American, provide drug coverage for all, and give insurance workers who would lose their jobs funds for retraining or job placement programs.

In today's America, health care for all is unlikely to happen. In the 2002 election, the medical industry contributed $95,180,336, mostly to conservative candidates.[31] Following the election, CEO's from the world's biggest drug companies met at Washington's Dulles Airport for a quick meeting to discuss the returns they wanted on the millions they successfully invested in candidates.[32] A short time later they had their prize: Congress passed the administration's massively wasteful elderly drug bill, ensuring undeserved billions in drug profits for years to come.

Conservatives have always discouraged a move to universal single-payer coverage by playing on public fears of big government, long waiting times for medical procedures, and lack of choice among doctors and other health care providers. But if problems with a single-payer system were as real as the insurance industry claims, why are none of the other rich democracies adopting the American model? Why do consumers in Canada and the United Kingdom express much greater satisfaction with their systems than Americans do, as seen in Chart 2.4?

Consumer Satisfaction In Three Countries

Chart 2.4 [33]

	Did not fill a prescription due to cost	Did not get recommended test, treatment, or follow-up due to cost	Needed dental care but did not see a dentist due to cost	Had a medical problem but did not visit doctor due to cost	Problems paying medical bills
Canada					
below-average income	22%	9%	42%	9%	14%
above-average income	7%	4%	15%	3%	3%
United Kingdom					
below-average income	7%	4%	20%	4%	4%
above-average income	7%	1%	19%	2%	2%
United States					
below-average income	39%	36%	51%	36%	35%
above-average income	18%	14%	24%	15%	11%

For 60 years, conservatives have fought and won many fights for the insurance industry, battles the companies could never have won if they were conducted in full public view. It took Lyndon Johnson's War on Poverty in 1965, bitterly opposed by conservatives, to win health services for millions of citizens under his revolutionary Medicare and Medicaid programs.

When the Clinton administration proposed a modest overhaul of the system in 2003, the medical industry charged that "big government will control your health care." Big government already is deeply involved in health care. It insures 42 million elderly through Medicare,[34] and pays for much of the care to 52 million disabled, poor, or working families served by the state-administered Medicaid program.[35] These programs are essential to the health and security of a third of the population. They could easily be consolidated into a universal health insurance plan that efficiently serves all Americans.

In the meantime, there were bills in the Congress to cover all nine million of the remaining uninsured children. The cost? About $25 billion—nearly equal to the 2006 tax breaks that go to the U.S. households with annual incomes over $300,000.[36] Other bills introduced to insure every American would produce economic benefits of $65 billion to $130 billion annually,[37] and save an estimated 18,000 lives.[38]

Conservatives derailed committee hearings on all of these bills and prevented debate on the floor of Congress as well. According to a 2005 national poll, this obstructionism does not reflect the will of the public. By a three to one margin, the public preferred health insurance for all of the nation's children instead of further tax breaks.[39]

Nobody is proposing that government workers deliver health care services. But just like the other rich democracies, the federal government could efficiently pay for and administer medical insurance—just the way it's done successfully around the globe.

In 2004, President Bush declared that "America's children must also have a healthy start in life...We will not allow a lack of attention...to stand between these children and the health care they need."[40] In 2006, in order to pay for more tax breaks, the President called for a budget which would have:

- Put 200,000 children at risk of losing health insurance coverage.[41]

- Created health savings accounts favoring high-income families.[42]

- Frozen funding for the Maternal and Child Health Block Grant.[43]

- Cut Medicaid another $13 billion over five years.[44]

- Eliminated $735 million for special education for children with disabilities.[45]

- Eliminated funding for the Safe and Drug Free Schools Program.[46]

- Eliminated the Preventive Care Block Grant for under-served populations.[47]

- Cut the Community Services Block Grant which includes funds for the disabled.[48]

- Cut Section 8 Housing for the low-income disabled.[49]

Is cutting health services to the neediest citizens an example of compassionate conservatism?

Uninsured Citizens On The Rise

Health insurance for all Americans is clearly on a downward trend: as seen in Chart 2.5, about one million people were added to the uninsured each year after conservatives took full control of the federal government in 2001. At the same time, skyrocketing medical costs vacuumed up resources that could be spent on critically needed investments in our children.

We can do a lot better than this.

Chart 2.5 [50]

Year	Number of Uninsured
2000	39,804,000
2001	41,207,000
2002	43,574,000
2003	44,961,000
2004	45,306,000
2005	46,577,000

Now let's look at a few health-related charts to see the effect of conservative ideology on its epicenter, Texas, and on other states where anti-government/ anti-tax philosophy prevails.

Conservative Health Policy at Work in Texas
Chart 2.6

	U.S.	Texas	Texas Rank
Percent of children uninsured [51]	15.7%	24.6%	1
Percentage of Fully-immunized Two-Year-Olds [52]	84%	75%	47
Teenage Birth Rate (live births/ 1000 mothers aged 15-19) [53]	43	64.4	2

Texas has the highest percent of uninsured children, the 4th worst rate of immunizing two-year-olds, and a teen birth rate 50% higher than the national average.

There are more uninsured children in Texas than in these 26 states combined.

Chart 2.7[54]

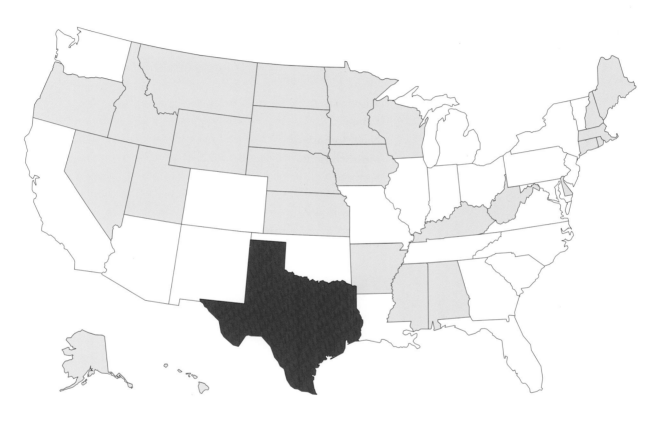

State	Uninsured	State	Uninsured	State	Uninsured
Alabama	57,000	Maine	22,000	Oregon	90,000
Alaska	15,000	Massachusetts	67,000	Rhode Island	19,000
Arkansas	73,000	Minnesota	76,000	South Dakota	16,000
Connecticut	68,000	Mississippi	86,000	Utah	94,000
Delaware	24,000	Montana	31,000	West Virginia	28,000
Hawaii	18,000	Nebraska	26,000	Wisconsin	97,000
Idaho	46,000	Nevada	93,000	Wyoming	15,000
Iowa	34,000	New Hampshire	17,000	Texas	1,244,000
Kansas	48,000	North Dakota	13,000		
Kentucky	68,000				

Yellow states combined:
Total Child Population: **15,432,000**
Number of Uninsured Children: **1,241,000**

Texas:
Total Child Population: **6,477,000**
Number of Uninsured Children: **1,244,000**

Uninsured Children 2003-2005 (Average)

Top States vs. Bottom States • Chart 2.8 [55]

Rank	State	% of Children Uninsured
1	Minnesota	8.7
2	Hawaii	9.5
3	Iowa	9.8
4	Wisconsin	10.3
5	Maine	10.4
5	New Hampshire	10.4
7	Massachusetts	10.7
7	Vermont	10.7
9	Kansas	10.9
10	Connecticut	11.0
	Median Top 10	**10.4**
41	Alaska	17.8
42	Arizona	18.1
43	Nevada	18.4
44	Louisiana	18.7
44	Montana	18.7
46	California	18.8
47	Oklahoma	19.5
48	Florida	19.6
49	New Mexico	21.1
50	Texas	24.6
	Median Bottom 10	**18.8**

Children in the bottom 10 states are 1.8 times as likely to be uninsured as children in the top 10. A Texas child is 2.8 times as likely to be uninsured as a child in Minnesota.

Low Birth Weight

Top States vs. Bottom States • Chart 2.9 [56]

Rank	State	Percent of infants born underweight
1	Alaska	6.0
1	Washington	6.0
3	Oregon	6.1
4	Minnesota	6.2
4	New Hampshire	6.2
6	Idaho	6.5
6	Maine	6.5
6	North Dakota	6.5
6	Utah	6.5
10	California	6.6
Median Top 10		**6.35**
41	Colorado	9.0
41	Georgia	9.0
41	North Carolina	9.0
44	Maryland	9.1
45	Delaware	9.4
45	Tennessee	9.4
47	Alabama	10.0
48	South Carolina	10.1
49	Louisiana	10.7
50	Mississippi	11.4
Median Bottom 10		**9.4**

Infants in the bottom 10 states are 50% more likely to be born underweight. Infants in Mississippi are almost twice as likely to be born underweight as Alaska or Washington infants.

Washington and Pennsylvania are not included in this ranking due to lack of data.

Prenatal Care

Top States vs. Bottom States • Chart 2.10 [57]*

Rank	State	Percent of births to women receiving late or no prenatal care
1	New Hampshire	1.1
1	Rhode Island	1.1
3	Connecticut	1.5
4	Vermont	1.6
5	Maine	1.7
6	Iowa	2
6	Massachusetts	2
8	Missouri	2.2
8	Minnesota	2.2
10	West Virginia	2.3
Median Top 10		**1.85**
37	Colorado	4.4
40	New York	4.5
41	Texas	4.7
41	New Jersey	4.7
43	Oklahoma	4.8
44	South Carolina	4.9
45	Alaska	5.2
46	Nevada	6.4
47	Arizona	7.3
48	New Mexico	8.1
Median Bottom 10		**4.85**

Women in the bottom 10 states are more than twice as likely to receive inadequate prenatal care as women in the top 10 states. Women in New Mexico are more than 7 times as likely to miss out as women in New Hampshire.

Infant Mortality Rate

Top States vs. Bottom States • Chart 2.11 [58]

Rank	State	Number of Deaths of Infants per 1,000 Live Births
1	New Hampshire	4.0
2	Minnesota	4.6
3	Massachusetts	4.8
4	Maine	4.9
5	Utah	5.0
5	Vermont	5.0
7	California	5.2
8	Connecticut	5.4
8	Nebraska	5.4
10	Iowa	5.6
Median Top 10		**5**
40	North Carolina	8.2
42	South Carolina	8.3
43	Georgia	8.5
43	Michigan	8.5
45	Alabama	8.7
45	Arkansas	8.7
47	Louisiana	9.3
47	Tennessee	9.3
49	Delaware	9.4
50	Mississippi	10.7
Median Bottom 10		**8.7**

Children born in the bottom 10 states are 74% more likely to die before their first birthday than children in the top 10. Infants born in Mississippi are more than 2 times as likely to die as infants in New Hampshire.

Child Deaths

Top States vs. Bottom States • Chart 2.12 [59]

Rank	State	Deaths per 100,000 Children 1-14
1	New Hampshire	12
2	Massachusetts	13
3	Connecticut	14
3	Delaware	14
3	Rhode Island	14
6	New Jersey	15
7	New York	16
7	Vermont	16
9	Hawaii	18
9	Minnesota	18
Median Top 10		**14.5**
41	Idaho	26
42	Alabama	27
42	Arkansas	27
44	Louisiana	28
45	New Mexico	29
45	Oklahoma	29
47	Mississippi	33
48	South Dakota	36
49	Wyoming	37
50	Alaska	38
Median Bottom 10		**29**

A child in the bottom 10 states is twice as likely to die by the age of 14 as a child in the top 10. Alaska children are more than 3 times as likely to die by the age of 14 as New Hampshire children.

Teen Deaths

Top States vs. Bottom States • Chart 2.13 [60]

Rank	State	Deaths per 100,000 Teens 15-19
1	Connecticut	40
2	New Jersey	42
3	New Hampshire	46
4	New York	48
5	Massachusetts	51
6	Maine	53
6	Vermont	53
8	Hawaii	54
8	Washington	54
10	Michigan	55
	Median Top 10	**52**
41	Wyoming	85
41	North Dakota	85
43	Nevada	87
44	Alabama	89
44	Mississippi	89
46	West Virginia	90
47	Louisiana	96
48	New Mexico	97
49	Montana	104
50	Alaska	105
	Median Bottom 10	**89.5**

A teenager in the bottom 10 states is 72% more likely to die prematurely as a teen in the top 10. An Alaska teenager is more than twice as likely to die as a Connecticut teenager.

These charts dramatically illustrate that where one lives can be a major factor in life choices and outcomes. Generally, the top states are blue—meaning more taxes and more government-supported health, social, and education programs, plus stronger regulations on quality of care issues and greater adherence to national standards. Red states overwhelmingly populate the bottom 10 rankings, including categories literally pertaining to life and death. A decades-long anti-government and anti-tax ideology prevailed in many of these states.

3. CHILD ABUSE
A DARK SIDE OF AMERICA...

In October, 1984, I opened the morning paper and learned that four-year-old Angela Palmer died after her mother's psychotic live-in boyfriend placed her in a hot kitchen oven. As commissioner of Maine's Department of Human Services, I had the official responsibility for child protection.

Maine citizens were plunged into a state of shock. In the aftermath of blame and explanation that followed, the governor, my boss, asked me why this child was allowed to remain with her parents after an investigation found they failed to meet her basic needs. Further, he asked, why shouldn't the state simply take custody of all children in similar circumstances?

I reminded the governor that thousands of Maine children lived in marginal homes, and no child had been killed for several years. Should the state wrench thousands of children from their homes in the hope that it might prevent a single death? Besides, I told him, few people were willing to bring deeply distressed children permanently into their homes. We both agreed that a lot more should be done to prevent and treat child abuse in the first place.

But the daily child abuse and neglect stories which appear in local newspapers across the United States tell us our nation has much more to do. Thankfully, few stories end as heartbreakingly as young Angela's. But with nearly three million reports of abuse to child protection agencies each year, it isn't surprising that polls show deep public concern about the problem—and a willingness to spend more to treat and prevent it. But many state and federal elected officials have concluded that child abuse is not a political priority, so it remains a dark underside of U.S. culture. Still, the problem claims the lives of thousands, ruins the lives of millions, and costs taxpayers more than $20 billion annually for child protection and foster care alone.[1] Child abuse also causes another hundred billion to be spent on related issues of crime, prisons, mental health, special education, medical care, and drug abuse.[2]

In 2004 at least 1,490
children died as a result
of abuse or neglect at home.
The true number may be
double that figure because
some states maintain data
in a way that masks the
true figure.[3]

- 81% of the fatalities were
  children under age four—
  mostly infants and toddlers

- 79% involved a parent
  as perpetrator

IN 2004:

- 872,000 children were the victims of confirmed abuse or neglect.[4]

  - 62% of these children were neglected— they did not receive proper food, clothing, shelter, hygiene, education, medical care or protection.

  - 18% were physically abused.

  - 10% were sexually abused.

  - 7% suffered from emotional abuse.

  - 15% suffered from other mistreatment such as abandonment, threats, and congenital drug addiction.[5]

- At least 50% of child abuse and neglect cases are associated with alcohol or drug abuse by parents.[6]

- One of every seven child victims of sexual assault reported to law enforcement agencies was under age six.[7]

- Among rape victims less than 12 years old, 90% knew the offender.[8]

- One in five adult women and one in ten adult men report having been sexually abused in childhood.[9]

As alarming as these numbers are, the actual number of child abuse and neglect incidents may run three times higher than official statistics, according to federal studies.

Despite the suffering of so many children, and despite the role that child abuse plays in future crime, poor education performance, failed relationships, and mental illness, there has been almost no national progress in either its prevention or treatment in the 37 years that I've been directly involved in this issue. It was a terrible problem when I first witnessed it in the early 1970's and it's a terrible problem today. Too many children are born to parents completely unprepared for their new responsibility. Too many child welfare workers have hugely excessive caseloads, and too few programs exist to help the families most at risk.

It's not an easy problem to solve. Half of the calls I'd get on child abuse as human services commissioner were from people who thought we had not done enough to protect a child. The other half, regarding the same case, would complain that our involvement was threatening the existence of the family. Both sides had a point, and it's this gray area that makes the work so daunting. If cases were black and white, decision-making would be easy. The reason it's so difficult is because the consequences can be enormous: leave a child in harm's way, or exercise powerful state authority which can result in the termination of parental rights. Child abuse laws properly err on the side of children. Lawmakers long ago decided that the full force of government can intervene on behalf of a child. The laws treat the parental role as one of stewardship, not ownership: parents are not free to do with their children as they wish.

So what's my quarrel with compassionate conservatism when it comes to child abuse? Aren't conservatives as concerned about children being harmed as anyone else? Yes, it goes without saying. However, conservative ideological distaste for government spending and taxes creates big problems.

In many states and in Congress, conservative lawmakers have tried unsuccessfully to weaken the government's power in child abuse cases.

For example, some have tried to make it a crime to report a child abuse case, even in good faith, if the allegation proves to be invalid. In Congressional testimony, I once got into a heated debate with a Texas representative who was convinced that all child abuse cases are private family matters that can be 'handled' by local churches.

At the same time, other conservative lawmakers pushed for an end to sometimes lengthy court procedures in child abuse cases. Their legislative success in expediting the termination of parental rights contributed to the rising numbers of children in out-of-home care, now approaching 525,000.[10] This approach benefited some children, particularly those adopted by loving families. But it also harmed many others, unnecessarily breaking up families because timely services were not available.

Per capita state spending in child welfare varies by as much as 700% from the highest spending state to the lowest.

Child welfare work is labor intensive. It requires mature workers with extensive training to properly assess a family's complicated situation. The goal should always be to protect children from harm and to strengthen families. Some states, and most of the other rich democracies, do this preventive work very successfully. It's not that we don't know how to prevent child abuse; it's that we haven't committed the funds—that is, the staff and services—to reach all the families that need help. Conservatives at the state and federal level, ideologically opposed to government intervention in the first place, often refuse to provide adequate funds. Here is where a strong public/private partnership can come into play. Public agencies can reserve their powers for the most severe cases, and private agencies, with adequate public funding, can take responsibility for the many more cases which do not require the full force of government to protect children and strengthen families.

But a comprehensive approach is lacking in most states across the country. At present, the amount of help a child receives is largely an accident of geography; some states do a much better job than others. As can be seen in Chart 3.1, the difference in spending to protect children between blue states versus red states is dramatic.

Per Capita Child Welfare Spending

Top States vs. Bottom States • Chart 3.1[11]

State	Total Child Welfare Expenditures for State Fiscal Year (Millions)	Total Population (Thousands of People)	Per Capita Child Welfare Expenditures (Nearest Dollar)
Rhode Island	$167	1,037	$161
New York	$2,553	18,634	$137
Alaska	$82	636	$129
Minnesota	$622	4,959	$125
California	$3,969	35,055	$113
Maine	$144	1,279	$112
Vermont	$67	601	$112
Iowa	$317	2,851	$111
Illinois	$1,373	12,391	$111
Pennsylvania	$1,281	11,958	$107
Median Top 10			**$113**
Florida	$766	16,990	$45
Georgia	$386	8,581	$45
New Mexico	$77	1,863	$41
Connecticut	$140	3,389	$41
North Carolina	$314	8,270	$38
Texas	$825	21,912	$38
Idaho	$50	1,360	$37
Nevada	$78	2,301	$34
Arkansas	$68	2,676	$25
Mississippi	$57	2,805	$20
Median Bottom 10			**$38**

The top 10 states fund child welfare programs at nearly 3 times the level of the bottom 10. Child welfare spending in Rhode Island is more than 8 times Mississippi's.

No states are in full compliance with federal child welfare standards.[12] Recent federal reviews of state performance, ignored by the press, confirm that many gaps exist in the ability of states to protect children, to provide quality foster care, and to move children to adoption when appropriate. No state is doing enough. An increase in spending would alleviate many problems. All cases of reported abuse could be properly evaluated. Case loads of social workers could be reduced, and more staff could receive ongoing training. Prevention services would be available to families at risk. The quality and quantity of foster homes could be increased. Coordination between law enforcement and child welfare officials could be greatly improved.

Because child welfare work requires a lot of staff and is emotionally stressful, a critical consideration in every state is whether highly trained social workers can be retained. One consideration is compensation. In some states the starting salary for caseworkers is as low as $23,000, while the top of the scale for veteran caseworkers is only $35,000.[13]

When trained staff and adequate services are available, children are more likely to be protected and abusive parents are more likely to learn how to care for their children. The alternative? Children at higher risk of injury or death and families more likely to fail.

It doesn't need to be this way. The good news is that we know a lot about healthy child development. Many countries have applied this knowledge and consequently have much less child abuse, one measure of which can be seen in Chart 3.2 comparing U.S. deaths from child abuse to other rich democracies.

Child Maltreatment Deaths *per 100,000 Children*

Chart 3.2 [14]

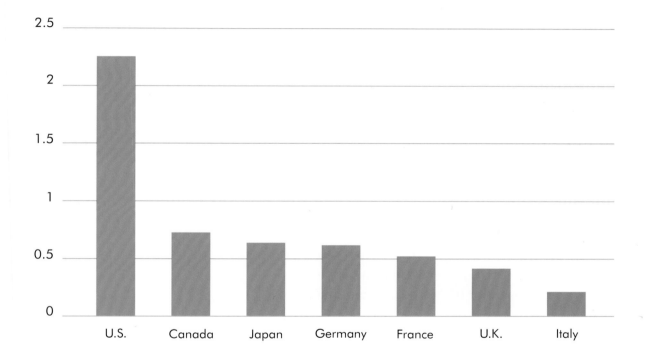

The U.S. child abuse death rate is 3 times higher than the next of the rich democracies, Canada's, and is 11 times higher than Italy's.

The key to child abuse prevention is to help potentially abusive parents with their responsibilities, and the earlier the better. Several states have applied these lessons as well. Their children experience less abuse than children in other states. When children in these states are abused, their families are much more likely to receive help.

We know how to identify families at risk, even while women are pregnant or during the hospital stay at birth. We also know there are children whose survival is at risk because they live in dangerous, abusive circumstances. These children should be permanently separated from their birth families as soon as possible and placed with families willing to care for and protect them. Fortunately, the number of families who can't be helped is very small. And fortunately, the vast majority of parents who have abused or neglected their children want to do well by them. These parents can change their behavior, sometimes with a little help, more often with a lot.

Many citizens would like to see all abused children removed from their families, placed in foster care, and adopted. While it's true that the great majority of children who enter foster care are protected from further harm at home, there is no guarantee that the experience will be a positive one for them. While we are grateful to foster parents who open their homes, many children cannot be matched with foster parents trained for their special needs. Even when they are, many

children would like nothing more than to return home, even to abusive parents, because of the strong need for family. But many can never return home because their parents may be mentally ill, severely addicted, in prison or dead.

One of the sad consequences of our compromised child welfare system is that every year about 20,000 teens ages 18 and 19, now legally adults, leave foster care with no place to go.[15] They were never adopted and their parents are not a resource for them. Most of them will never experience the support and education that gives middle class children a safe place to learn and experiment as they reach adulthood.

Young adults graduating from foster care often have a rough time living independently. One study found that within two to four years:[16]

- only 54% had completed high school

- less than half had jobs

- 25% had experienced homelessness

- 30% had no health care

- 60% of the girls had given birth

In a Wisconsin study, 18 percent of former foster youth experienced incarceration after leaving foster care.[17] In a Nevada study, 41 percent reported spending at least one night in jail, and 55 percent reported not having health insurance.[18]

Child abuse is overwhelmingly concentrated among the poorest families. In one study, children in families with income less than $15,000 were 22 times more likely to be abused or neglected than those in families making over $30,000.[19] Abuse occurs in families from all socioeconomic ranks, but lands hardest on children in the poorest families, where early parenthood, violence, mental illness, substance abuse, imprisonment, unemployment, low education, and poor housing wreak havoc on families. Many abused children who get help, perhaps most, are resilient enough to overcome this history. But for many others, the outcome is predictable: when childhood goes wrong, adulthood goes wrong, and the sad story of abuse will repeat itself from one generation of troubled families to the next.*

The United States has a long way to go to provide the kind of family supports which keep child abuse rates low and that are available to almost all parents in the other rich democracies. These include higher tax deductions for dependents, child care, comprehensive health care, children's allowances, paid parental leave, visiting nurses, school-based health and social services, and more. These measures are unlikely to draw much political attention in the United States because children can't vote and their usually poor or low-income parents mostly don't.

It is costly to provide proper treatment for an abused child. When elected officials see no political advantage or disadvantage to programs that help abused children, then child welfare administrators get the message not to ask for more resources.

While stories about child abuse are frequently reported in local papers, the national press generally limits its coverage to sensational child deaths. There is virtually no press coverage of the federal government's role in the prevention of child abuse. And it is a rare member of Congress who speaks to the issue, even though the federal government provides nearly half of the funds in the child welfare system, provides most of the statutory framework for state child welfare laws, and is obligated by federal law to evaluate state performance and to hold states accountable.

* Maltreated children are subject to serious health and mental problems: developmental and neurological disorders, delayed growth, lower IQ's, learning disabilities, mental retardation, cerebral palsy, and asthma. As they grow older, they are likely to have emotional and sexual problems, abuse drugs or alcohol, have impaired emotional and social abilities, and be candidates to commit crimes.

While all abuse and neglect is injurious, child sexual abuse is particularly troubling. The laws meant to protect children and punish perpetrators often fail:

"An undetermined, but significant number of children who have been sexually assaulted or otherwise sexually violated by adults, and whose plight has been brought to the attention of local and state authorities, are not receiving sufficient protection or assistance and, in fact, may still be living with those individuals who perpetrated the violation."[20]

These words come from a study I directed for a state legislature in the 90's, but they apply to most of the states in which I've worked. I routinely encountered a weak response to child sex abuse cases throughout the criminal justice system. I don't believe that the successful criminal prosecution and conviction rate of child sex abuse cases confirmed by government child protection agencies exceeds 10 to 20 percent in most states. This means that many offenders are able to repeat their predatory behavior over and over.

A nine-year-old mildly mentally retarded girl is confirmed by the child protection agency to have been sexually abused. The perpetrator is believed to be a 40-year-old male who lives in the home. The agency asks the police to arrest the suspected offender in order to strengthen its request to a judge that he be ordered to leave the home. This would protect the child and allow her to remain at school and with her family. The district attorney says the evidence is not strong enough to prosecute. Faced with the prospect that the offender will remain in the same house as the child, the child protection agency asks the court to place her in foster care. The court grants custody and the child is moved to a home 70 miles away with the only foster parents trained to deal with her mental deficiencies and sexual abuse. The girl comes to believe that her loss of home and school is punishment for "allowing" herself to be abused. Her subsequent depression and poor self-image eventually lead to early sexual behavior. She drops out of school to have a child at 15 and another at 17. Her life chances are declining sharply. She self-medicates with alcohol and then illicit drugs. Strange men come in and out of her home, creating an atmosphere that is not safe for her daughters. She is sent to prison at age 25 for further drug offenses. Her daughters are placed in foster homes. They experience depression and poor self-image…

Where were the conservatives in the administration and recent Congresses when it came to protecting children from abuse and neglect? Mostly, they were nowhere.

Some members of Congress comforted themselves by sending staff to occasional briefings on the topic of child abuse. They even may have tweaked an existing law or two. But on balance, their recent actions on taxes, health, and social programs reduced spending for a broad array of already inadequate safety net services that protect children, leaving more of them at risk of abuse.

Legislation with the muscle and money to help abused children was regularly introduced in recent Congresses, but was allowed to sit in committees for years. The committee chairs did not schedule hearings on these bills, so they did not come to the floor of Congress for a vote. The conservatives who dominated the administration and Congress preferred to debate such "family values" issues as same-sex marriage, flag-burning, and whether to allow the national anthem to be sung in Spanish.

The children in our examples had to look elsewhere for help and protection. Unless a new Congress makes greater investments, child abuse and neglect will continue at epidemic proportions in the richest of the rich democracies.

Total Daily Costs of Child Abuse and Neglect in the United States are More than $257 Million

Chart 3.3[21]

Direct Costs	Estimated Daily Cost
Health Care System	
- Hospitalization	$17,001,082
- Chronic Health Problems	$8,186,185
- Mental Health Care System	$1,164,686
Child Welfare System	$39,452,054
Law Enforcement	$67,698
Judicial System	$934,725
Total Direct Costs	**$66,806, 430**

Indirect Costs	Estimated Daily Cost
Special Education	$612,624
Mental Health and Health Care	$12,678,455
Juvenile Delinquency	$24,124,086
Lost Productivity to Society	$1,797, 260
Total Indirect Costs	**$190,938,452**

How have anti-government/anti-tax policies helped Texas children?

Chart 3.4[22]

	Texas Rank	Texas Children
Child Abuse Deaths	1	212

Child Welfare Protection[23] vs. Leisure Spending,[24] United States 2002

Chart 3.5

Total Child Welfare Protection Expenditures	$22,156,246,128
Total Consumer Spending on Alcohol	$116,000,000,000
Total Consumer Spending on Spectator Recreation	$34,800,000,000
Total Consumer Spending on Tobacco	$88,200,000,000

A 1% shift in spending from alcohol, spectator recreation, and tobacco to child protection would generate almost $2.5 billion—a sum that would prevent thousands of children from being abused, neglected, raped, or killed.

Child Abuse Fatalities 2004

Top States vs. Bottom States • Chart 3.6[25]

Rank	State	Total Child Fatalities	Fatalities per 100,000 Children
1	New Hampshire	0	0
1	North Dakota	0	0
1	Vermont	0	0
4	Nevada	2	0.33
5	Washington	7	0.47
6	Delaware	1	0.52
7	Maine	2	0.71
8	Minnesota	10	0.81
9	Massachusetts	12	0.82
10	Wisconsin	12	0.84
	Median Top 10		**0.495**
41	Illinois	85	2.62
42	Colorado	35	2.97
43	West Virginia	12	3.12
44	Texas	212	3.38
45	Wyoming	4	3.42
46	Missouri	48	3.47
47	Kentucky	38	3.88
48	Georgia	98	4.2
49	Oklahoma	39	4.54
50	Indiana	77	4.81
	Median Bottom 10		**3.445**

Children in the bottom states are 7 times as likely to die from abuse and neglect as children in the top states. Children in Indiana are almost 15 times more likely to die from abuse or neglect as those in Nevada.

Note: Michigan, Alaska and North Carolina did not provide data, and are not considered here.

4. PRISONS
A REFLECTION OF FAILED SOCIAL POLICY

My 59-year-old sister-in-law is now halfway through a 16-year sentence in federal prison, serving time for a first-offense white collar crime. She writes that one of the hardest things for her in prison is listening to mothers at night crying for their children. The prisoners she serves time with are mostly poor, uneducated, and Black or Latina. Many have been convicted of crimes related to check and credit card fraud, or to drugs.

U.S. prison populations continue to explode, rising from 338,000 in 1970 to more than 2.2 million in 2003.[1] That's an increase of nearly 700 percent in the number of Americans locked up in little more than a generation. Imprisonment has become a leading U.S. social policy—perhaps the leading U.S. social policy—to address the unchecked problems of substance abuse, poverty, mental illness, and educational failure. It's also harming the millions of children who have a parent in prison.

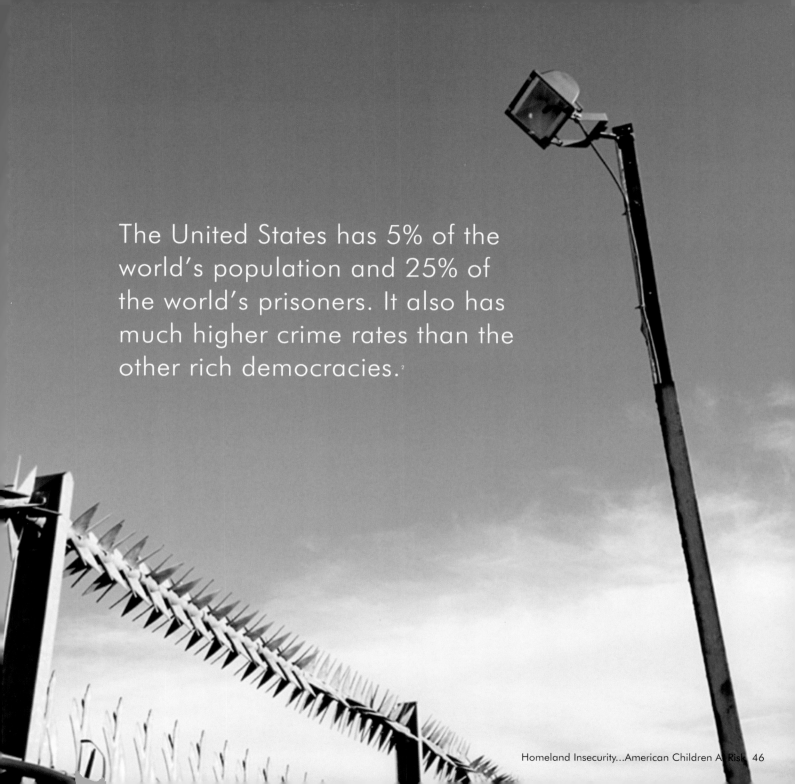

The United States has 5% of the world's population and 25% of the world's prisoners. It also has much higher crime rates than the other rich democracies.[2]

- The U.S. incarceration rate is more than six times the United Kingdom's and 12 times Japan's.

- The United States has a far greater reliance on incarceration, (Chart 4.1) but it is no deterrent to violence: the U.S. homicide rate is almost three times that of the United Kingdom, and more than five times that of Japan.

- Nor has the high U.S. incarceration rate meant lower firearms-related deaths than those of the other rich democracies: they are more than double France's and 113 times Japan's. (Chart 4.2)

Incarceration and Homicide
Chart 4.1

Prison Population per 100,000 people [3]	G7 Nation	Homicides per 100,000 People [4]
724	United States	5.62
114	United Kingdom	2.03
107	Canada	1.67
97	Germany	1.11
97	Italy	1.12
88	France	1.84
60	Japan	1.10

Firearm Deaths

Chart 4.2[5]

Country	Year	Firearm Deaths	Rate/100,000
Japan	1997	83	0.1
United Kingdom	1999	197	0.3
Germany	1999	1201	1.5
Italy	1997	1171	2.0
Canada	1997	1034	3.4
France	1998	2964	5.0
United States	1998	30,419	11.3

Indeed, the soaring rate of imprisonment in America has almost no correlation to the U.S. crime rate. As seen in Chart 4.3, states with incarceration rates lower than the national average had bigger drops in crime during the study period than states with incarceration rates higher than the national average.

Changes in incarceration and crime rates for states

Chart 4.3[6]

Grouped by above average and below average increases in incarceration, 1991-1996

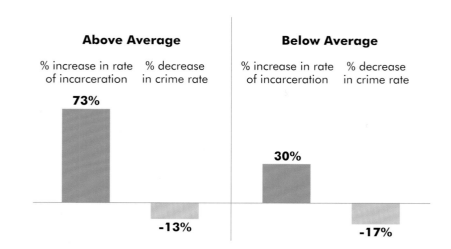

	Above Average		Below Average	
	% increase in rate of incarceration	% decrease in crime rate	% increase in rate of incarceration	% decrease in crime rate
	73%	-13%	30%	-17%

To this apparent contradiction, add the fact that more than half of all prisoners are serving time for drug-related offenses.[7] This raises a big question about the wisdom of our prison policies when we consider the widespread economic and social damage they create.

For nearly thirty years conservative ideology has shaped U.S. prison policy, which consists of little more than to lock up more people and lock them up longer. There is virtually no political or media discussion about our soaring incarceration rate. Most moderate and liberal politicians are terrified to even bring up the topic because they fear being labeled soft on crime. Press attention is largely confined to reporting on brutal crimes and the trials of high profile individuals and rarely examines the nearly invisible network of thousands of prisons and jails.

The prison population is overwhelmingly poor, uneducated, and disproportionately minority. Once locked up, there is little hope that the substance abuse common among offenders will be treated, or that education and job training will be provided for the hundreds of thousands of prisoners who re-enter society each year.

One study after another shows a high correlation between problems in childhood, such as abuse, poor parenting or mental illness, and incarceration. According to ChildHelpUSA, for instance, more than one-third of women prisoners reported being abused as children, compared with twelve to seventeen percent in the general population. About fourteen percent of male inmates reported abuse compared with five to eight percent of men in the general population.[8]

Childhood trauma never excuses a criminal act. People in the end must accept responsibility for their behavior. But early trauma can explain how bad behavior is manufactured. It can begin in utero when a fetus is assaulted by the mother's substance abuse or it can start when a toddler is victimized by a father's unrestrained violence.

The conservatives driving up the prison population, who favored tax cuts for the wealthy and deep cuts in government spending for social programs should reconsider—not because prisoners may deserve compassion, but because present policy guarantees that preventable crimes will be committed against innocent victims by individuals who, with help, could have followed a productive path instead.

We all know there are plenty of violent offenders who must remain in prison. We can agree that their crimes are so serious that justice and public safety require their removal from society. But it is wrong to use incarceration as a substitute for government policies that can combat and prevent poverty, mental illness, inadequate education, and substance abuse. Instead of funding social policies that have been proven to deter crime in other democracies, anti-government/anti-tax conservatives favor locking up more and more non-violent offenders who become a drag on our economy. And, high incarceration rates place a huge strain on state and federal budgets. Of approximately $40 billion spent on prisons in 2000, nearly $24 billion was spent to imprison 1.2 million non-violent offenders.[9] That's more than the combined federal budget for the Child Care and Development and Social Services Block Grants, adoption, child protection, and foster care programs. By 1995, states spent more building prisons than building colleges for the first time in U.S. history.[10]

Does it make sense for prisons to remain a growth industry, and for the stocks of private prison companies to be considered good long term investments? Whether intentional or not, that's what has happened in just one generation. It doesn't need to be this way. The situation could change if the political debate shifted from who's soft on crime to who's smart on crime.

Our failure to openly debate state and federal imprisonment policies dooms us to lock up ever more non-violent offenders who become a drag on our economy.

Prison policies affect everyone, but they weigh most heavily on African-Americans:

- More than nine percent of black males between 25 and 29 were in prison at the end of 2003—almost four times the Hispanic rate and seven times the white rate.[11]

- Black males comprise 44% of all inmates with sentences of more than a year, although they are only about 6.5% of the U.S. population.[12]

- One in three young black men is in prison, on probation or on parole, up from one in four a decade ago. In big U.S. cities, the rate is one in two.[13]

- The incarceration rate for black men is four times higher than the rate in South Africa during the apartheid era.[14]

- A black male born in 1991 has a 29% chance of being imprisoned at some point, compared to four percent for a white male.[15]

The imprisonment of black males has had a huge effect on black family formation, leaving single mothers in charge of millions of black families: 43 percent of black families are headed by women with no spouse present.[16] High incarceration rates for black males have a destabilizing effect on families and communities, and lead to higher rates of future criminal behavior and repeat offenses. A bad situation for the prisoner's family is often made worse when incarceration occurs far from home and community.[17] Upon release from prison, many convicts are barred from participating in the democratic process because many states deny former prisoners the right to vote. In some states re-entry into the job market is restricted by prohibitions on driving trucks or cutting hair, permanently condemning young ex-prisoners to dead-end, low-wage, and unstable employment. That's not exactly a prospect to boast about when seeking a marriage partner.

Imprisonment of women also has skyrocketed. There were 12,300 women in prison in 1980 and 104,848 in 2004—an increase of almost 900%.[18] Thirty-three percent of female prisoners are black.[19] Most women prisoners are poor. Their crimes often include credit card abuse or check forgery.[20] About one-third are serving mandatory sentences for drug offenses.[21] Almost 1.5 million children—58 percent under age 10—had a parent in prison in 1999.[22]

65% of women in state prisons have young children.[23]

In 1997, five percent of women entering prison were pregnant.[24]

The number of children with an imprisoned mother rose 98% in just eight years, to 126,100 in 1999.[25]

Seven percent of black children have a parent in jail, nearly nine times the rate for white children (0.8%). Hispanic children are almost three times as likely as white children to have an imprisoned parent.[26]

52

When parents are in jail, their children most often live with the remaining parent or with grandparents and other relatives. Many thousands also enter foster care.

In 1999, an estimated 721,000 prisoners left behind 1.5 million children.[27] These children are at increased risk for poor academic achievement, drug abuse, early pregnancy, juvenile delinquency—and imprisonment.

If we know anything about criminal behavior, it's that the roots of it take hold early. Evidence has grown showing that the very earliest years play a key role—even when the fetus is in the womb. Is the pregnancy a happy one? Is the mother smoking, doing drugs, drinking alcohol? Is she being physically or emotionally assaulted? Will the child be born to welcoming arms or to chaos? The early emotional state of a child helps determine its longer term sense of security or defensiveness, and its view of the world.

An informal study I directed in California in the 90's reinforced this view. The study measured the difference in arrest rates for children nine to 12 reported as abused or neglected versus the arrest rate for all other nine to 12 year olds. The difference was a stunning 67 times greater [6700%] arrest rate, confirming for me once again that bad behavior is largely manufactured, and that we know early which children are at greatest risk of getting deeper and deeper into trouble with the law.[28]

States and local jurisdictions vary widely in their response to young lawbreakers. Some are helpful. Most are not. Here's one example.

In 1992 I directed a Child Welfare League of America study of juvenile justice and child protection programs in Mississippi. We interviewed more than 600 people and visited numerous sites, including 15 local jails. We labeled the conditions we encountered as 'barbaric.' The Federal Department of Justice intervened and forced the state to improve its facilities. That was 14 years ago. Recently, the Department of Justice found that conditions in Mississippi's detention facilities were still harming children and youth.

Why Federal Monitoring Is Needed

1992 CWLA Mississippi Report[29]

- Abused children as young as nine years old are in county jails because there are no alternatives.

- Thirteen-year-old mentally ill and abused children, guilty of no crime, may spend as much as 60 days in local lock-ups, perhaps some of the time in a strait jacket, waiting for an opening at the state hospital.

- There were more than 1,000 substantiated cases of sexual abuse against children in 1991, yet only 40 convictions of offenders.

- Youths are sent to training schools—prisons for teenagers—for up to three or four months for crimes as minor as truancy—sometimes without legal representation.

- Large numbers of young people are expelled from school, often because of minor offenses, for as much as a full year with no alternative education program.

- A 14-year-old girl is led into jail in handcuffs behind her back, because of truancy, with no legal representation.

- A 13-year-old boy, abandoned by parents now in state penitentiaries, is in jail for running away and is not represented by an attorney.

- Hundreds of social workers, sheriffs, mental health providers, judges, and police officers expressed frustration about conditions they see every day which injure children and youth.

2003 Justice Report on Mississippi[30]

- Boys and girls were routinely hog-tied, shackled to poles or locked in restraint chairs for hours for minor infractions like talking in the cafeteria.

- Girls were made to run while carrying tires, boys while holding logs, sometimes to the point of vomiting or injury.

- Boys and girls were choked, slapped, beaten, and attacked with pepper spray.

- Girls who misbehaved… were stripped naked and left in a windowless, stifling cinder-block cell, with nothing but the concrete floor to sleep on and a hole in the floor for a toilet, for several days or even a week at a time. One girl had been locked in a bare cell for 114 straight days.

In 1992 While visiting 15 county jails in Mississippi, I interviewed a small 11-year-old boy locked behind a thick steel door. It was almost impossible to see through the cloudy plastic window. After I was let inside, I could barely see the boy under the light of a low watt single bulb.

"Why are you here?"
"Skipping school."
"Have you seen an attorney?"
"No."
"Where are your parents?"
"My dad is in prison."
"Your mom?"
"The last time I saw her was three years ago when she told me to get out of the car and then she drove away."

I asked the sheriff why this child was in his jail. At first he protested. Then, tears welling up in his eyes, he said there were no alternatives and he had to follow the court's order. I asked the judge why the boy did not have a lawyer as required by law. He said he also served as the county's lawyer and had to look out for their budget. On my way out the boy tapped on the glass and asked:

"Mister, can you please get me out of here?"
"We're trying," I said,
"We're trying."

These incidents took place at two Mississippi training schools for boys and girls under age 18 who are charged with offenses ranging from truancy, under-age drinking and smoking, up to homicide. The federal investigators reported that the schools were under-staffed and under-financed, employed poorly trained workers who physically and verbally abused the children in their care, and withheld education and basic medical care, all in violation of state and federal laws.[31]

Juvenile crime in the United States has declined steadily for more than a decade. The number of minors incarcerated in detention centers, however, has climbed along with incarceration rates for the general population.[32]

Chart 4.4

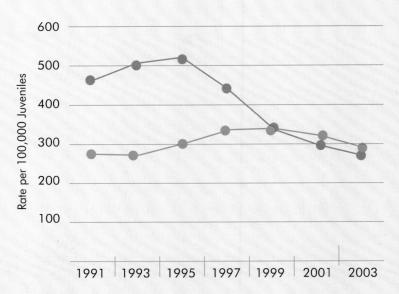

- Violent Crime Index
- Juvenile Incarceration Rate

On any given day, more than 134,000 juveniles are incarcerated in the United States.[33] Of these, about 14,000 are held in adult facilities, including 9100 in local jails and 5400 in adult prisons.[34]

Nearly 70 percent of the youths were detained for non-violent offenses, more than half were age 15 or under, and more than one-third were age 14 or less.[35] Almost 40,000 of the youths detained each year are arrested for offenses that would not be considered crimes if they were committed by adults.[36] These so-called status offenses include running away from home, violating curfews, underage smoking and drinking, and disorderly conduct.

Government programs aimed at strengthening families, mentoring disadvantaged youths, and counseling juvenile offenders have repeatedly shown a significant reduction in further criminal behavior, a drop in repeat arrests, and a decrease in mental health problems among troubled youths.[37]

In previous years, the President has spoken to the needs of delinquent youths, particularly young boys. His words have been comforting, but his budgets are reducing the chance to succeed for millions of young boys and girls.

Crime and Punishment in Texas
Chart 4.5

	U.S. Average	Texas	Texas Rank
Number of Executions [38]	1.2	19	1
Number of Adults Incarcerated [39]		168,105	1
Incarceration Rate [40]	5.91	10.73	3
Number of Women Incarcerated [41]		13,958	1
Crime Rate [42]	3824.3	5034.5	6

Texas executes more prisoners and imprisons more people than any other state, yet 44 states have lower crime rates. The charts which follow show that generally, the states which have the best outcomes for children have the lowest rates of crime and incarceration; conversely, states which show more bad outcomes for children tend to have larger rates of crime and incarceration.

Crime Rates

Top States vs. Bottom States • *Table 4.6* [43]

Rank	State	Overall Crime Rate per 100,000 inhabitants	Overall Child Well-being Rank
1	North Dakota	1996.0	9
2	South Dakota	2105.0	14
3	New Hampshire	2207.1	1
4	Vermont	2420.2	2
5	Maine	2513.1	11
6	New York	2640.2	22
7	West Virginia	2777.4	38
8	Kentucky	2782.6	42
9	New Jersey	2784.9	7
10	Pennsylvania	2826.1	16
	Median Top 10	**2576.7**	**16.2**
41	New Mexico	4885.0	48
42	Florida	4891.0	33
43	Oregon	4929.6	15
44	Tennessee	5001.7	46
45	Texas	5034.5	39
46	Hawaii	5047.2	21
47	Louisiana	5048.9	49
48	Washington	5193.0	17
49	South Carolina	5289.0	47
50	Arizona	5844.6	37
	Median Bottom 10	**5040.9**	**35.2**

Crime rates in the bottom 10 states are double those in the top 10. Arizona's crime rate is almost three times North Dakota's. Note that the states in the top 10 have an aggregate Child Well-being rank of 16.2, putting them in the top one-third of all states with respect to overall child well-being. The bottom 10 states have an aggregate score of 35.2, putting them in the bottom one-third of all states on child well-being. Conclusion: Taking good care of children is an effective crime-fighting strategy.

Incarceration Rates

Top States vs. Bottom States • Table 4.7 [44]

Rank	State	Prison Population	Incarcerated People per 1000 adults	Overall Child Well-being Rank
1	Maine	2,024	2.03	11
2	Massachusetts	10,144	2.14	10
3	Minnesota	8,758	2.35	4
4	New Hampshire	2,448	2.56	1
5	North Dakota	1,327	2.81	9
6	Nebraska	4,130	3.26	8
7	Washington	16,614	3.63	17
8	West Virginia	5,067	3.65	38
9	Utah	5,989	3.71	6
10	Iowa	8,525	3.93	5
Median Top 10			**3.04**	**10.9**
41	South Carolina	23,428	7.70	47
42	Alabama	25,887	7.78	43
43	Arizona	32,515	7.95	37
44	Georgia	51,104	8.14	44
45	Oklahoma	23,319	9.11	40
46	Alaska	4,554	10.16	35
47	Mississippi	20,983	10.19	50
48	Texas	168,105	10.73	39
49	Delaware	6,927	11.31	29
50	Louisiana	36,939	11.47	49
Median Bottom 10			**9.64**	**41.3**

Adults in the bottom 10 states are three times as likely to be incarcerated as adults in the top 10. Louisiana's incarceration rate is nearly six times Maine's. Note the poor Child Well-being ranking of the states with the highest incarceration rates and the favorable Child Well-being ranking of the states with the lowest incarceration rates. Again: taking care of children leads to less imprisonment.

Juvenile Incarceration

Top States vs. Bottom States • Table 4.8 [45]

Rank	State	**Custody Rate** per 100,000 juveniles (10+years old)
1	Vermont	72
2	Hawaii	97
3	New Hampshire	150
4	Mississippi	152
5	Maine	153
6	North Carolina	169
7	Maryland	181
8	Kentucky	185
9	New Jersey	199
10	Connecticut	210
Median Top 10		**161**
41	Alabama	351
42	Nevada	362
43	Delaware	364
44	Alaska	370
45	Louisiana	387
46	California	392
47	Indiana	415
48	Florida	452
49	South Dakota	564
50	Wyoming	606
Median Bottom 10		**390**

Juveniles in the bottom 10 states are almost two and a half times as likely to be incarcerated as juveniles in the top 10.
A Wyoming juvenile is more than eight times as likely to be incarcerated as a juvenile in Vermont.

5. CHILD POVERTY
LOOK AWAY, LOOK AWAY...

Driving home on a chilly October evening, I passed four figures walking along the highway. I turned the car around and met Mary, 25, and her three children, seven, eight, and nine years old. It was 11 p.m. She was wearing a white uniform and the children were in stocking-feet pajamas. I asked where they were going. "Work," she said. She was enroute to her 11 o'clock night shift as a nursing home aide. She didn't want to lose her job. She and the children had walked seven miles already and had eight more to go. Her husband was in prison. They lived with her father in a trailer. He was drunk that evening and refused to let her use his car or to watch the children, as he customarily did. I piled them into my car and took them to an all-night diner. I called the nursing home and arranged for the children to be left with a friend of Mary's. I then dropped Mary off at work.

Like many other single working mothers, Mary was living far below the poverty level and struggling mightily to get by. She also shared the kind of life experience commonly found among poor families: too-early parenthood, a spouse in prison, no child support, substance abuse, sub-standard housing, unreliable transportation, a physically challenging low-wage job, low educational achievement, and, yes, often poor judgment about many things. On the positive side, Mary, like most mothers, shared a commitment to do the right thing for her children, a willingness to learn, and a desire to work and become self-sufficient.

The next day, Mary's case got special attention from my office. With hands-on assistance from a social worker, affordable after-school care was arranged so that she could work the day shift and be home at night. A local church group gave her a small car loan and she put in an application for a partially subsidized, modest apartment in a safe neighborhood within walking distance of schools. Mary's children were enrolled in Medicaid and the family was accepted for the federal food stamp program. Mary applied for a scholarship at a technical school in a program that would raise her salary by $2 per hour—nearly a 40 percent increase over her near-minimum wage job. Within months, Mary had won her pay increase. She persuaded her father to attend

The highest child poverty rate in America—30%—is in the U.S. metropolitan area with the second-highest income, Washington D.C. In the world's most powerful capital, wretched poverty begins a few blocks from the Capitol where Congress, from 2001-2006, bestowed trillions in tax breaks on the wealthiest Americans.

Poverty Is Not
a Character Builder

"Poverty is associated with negative outcomes for children. It can impede children's cognitive development and their ability to learn. It can contribute to behavioral, social and emotional problems. [it]…can lead to poor health…[the risks]…are greatest among children who experience poverty when they are young and among children who experience persistent and deep poverty…"[2]

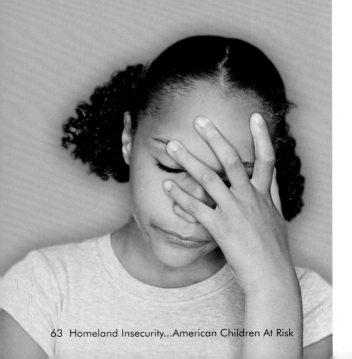

Alcoholics Anonymous. Her children were comforted by their new-found, albeit modest, security. Things were looking up.

Mary's family got the help it needed for a better future from programs subsidized by taxpayers, along with assistance from a local church and a local United Way agency. However, any social worker would tell you that Mary's situation was not as serious as many they encounter: neither parent had a mental or physical disability; the children were healthy; there was no history of child abuse or domestic violence. Any of those factors would have made Mary's situation far worse.

Does Mary bear responsibility for her predicament? Yes. Should she have had her first child at age 16? No. Should she have chosen a better husband? Yes. Graduated from high school? Yes.

Did the three children choose Mary as a parent? Do their life chances improve if Mary's do? Is it in their best interest for Mary to succeed? Does the community have a moral responsibility to help lift children—and their mothers and fathers—from poverty?

It's been decades since Congress had a serious debate about poverty. The welfare reform legislation of the 1990's was not about reducing child poverty. It was about reducing the number of families on the welfare rolls. And it has. In 1996 there were 4.4 million families on welfare. Today there are 1.9 million.[3] But there are still millions of children in working families living below the poverty level.

IN 2004:[*]

- 40 percent of America's 73 million children — 29.2 million — lived in low income families, 18% lived below the official poverty line.

- Although "only" 27% of white children lived in low income families, they were the largest group—40%—of low-income children.

- 61% of black children — 6.6 million — lived in low income families, 33% lived below the poverty line.

- 63% of Hispanic children — 8.9 million — lived in low income families, 29% lived below the poverty line.

- Although 81% of children lived in families where at least one parent worked full or part-time, 14 million children lived in families unable to provide enough food for all members.

- One survey estimated that 1.4 million children — 60% of them eight years old and younger — go through a period of homelessness at least once a year.[5]

- 81% of families who rent lived in areas where two full-time minimum wage workers cannot afford a two-bedroom apartment.[6]

* Low income [poverty] is defined as $40,000 [$20.000] for a family of four; $33,200 [$16,600] for a family of three; $26,400 [$13,200] for a family of two.

The Impact of Taxes and Transfers on Child Poverty

Chart 5.1[*7]

The U.S., the richest country in the world, has the second-worst child poverty rate (next to Mexico) among 26 rich countries. Other countries have lower poverty rates largely due to federal tax policies.

Child Poverty rates based on household incomes <u>after</u> government taxes and transfers

Child Poverty rates based on household incomes <u>before</u> government taxes and transfers

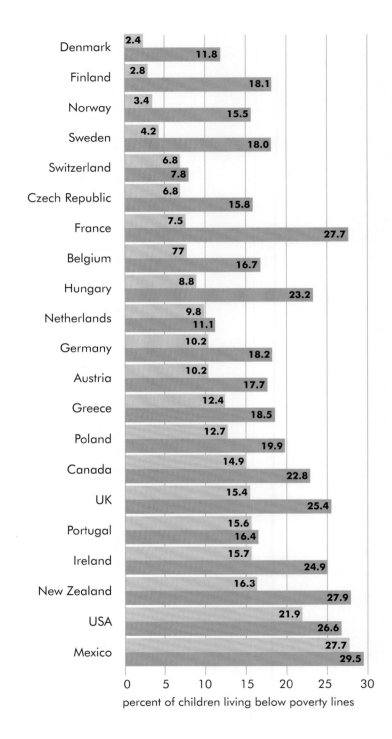

Country	after	before
Denmark	2.4	11.8
Finland	2.8	18.1
Norway	3.4	15.5
Sweden	4.2	18.0
Switzerland	6.8	7.8
Czech Republic	6.8	15.8
France	7.5	27.7
Belgium	77	16.7
Hungary	8.8	23.2
Netherlands	9.8	11.1
Germany	10.2	18.2
Austria	10.2	17.7
Greece	12.4	18.5
Poland	12.7	19.9
Canada	14.9	22.8
UK	15.4	25.4
Portugal	15.6	16.4
Ireland	15.7	24.9
New Zealand	16.3	27.9
USA	21.9	26.6
Mexico	27.7	29.5

percent of children living below poverty lines

* For the purpose of comparison, poverty is defined as a household with income below 50% of the national median.

Do we know how to reduce child poverty? We do. The Great Society initiatives of the mid-1960's, for example, helped knock back child poverty to a record low 14 percent by 1969.[8]

The other rich democracies also provide an example: their national anti-poverty policies reduce child poverty by a much greater percentage than our own modest efforts, as seen in Charts 5.1 and 5.2.

The Effectiveness of Government Intervention

Chart 5.2[9]

G7 Nation	Child Poverty Before Government Intervention	Child Poverty After Government Intervention	Percent Change
France	27.7%	7.5%	-72.92%
Germany	18.2%	10.2%	-43.96%
U.K.	25.4%	15.4%	-39.37%
Canada	22.8%	14.9%	-34.65%
Japan	NA	NA	NA
Italy	NA	NA	NA
U.S.	26.6%	21.9%	-17.67%

Most instructive, the U.S. government has achieved spectacular results in reducing elderly poverty rates. The drop is attributed to the guaranteed income provided by Social Security, which includes an annual cost of living adjustment, combined with guaranteed access to health care through Medicare and Medicaid, plus other federal programs. If similar programs were extended

to children and families, there also would be a dramatic drop in the child poverty rate. In 1959 the poverty rate for the elderly was 35.2 percent. Today it is 10.1 percent.[10]

The low senior poverty rate cannot be attributed to an increase in the elderly savings rate or a huge upsurge in the elderly workforce. It is mostly the result of federal programs, proving two things: federal policies that boost incomes work, and senior political power matters.

The stubbornly high children's poverty rate is not the result of parents who don't work hard enough; families today work more hours than before. It's mostly due to conservative federal policies that directed only modest funds to programs for children. These policies were directly related to the weak political power of children and families—especially the most distressed.

Conservatives took pains in recent decades to misrepresent the effectiveness of government poverty programs. They loudly proclaimed that we fought the poverty war and lost, and that only the private sector could improve the economic status of the poor. They ignored the fact that the numbers of poor are rising, despite the soaring stock market of recent years and huge new fortunes for the wealthy. In fact, real wages for 80 percent of American workers actually declined the last four years.[11]

Conservatives pointed to "trillions" spent on fighting the war on poverty, omitting the fact that most of the money went to Social Security and Medicare, mainly to benefit the middle-class elderly. They also ignored statistics which show low child poverty rates in the other rich democracies are the result of public, not private, policies.

U.S. federal spending is more than eight times greater per person for citizens over age 65 than for those under age 18. In 2000, federal spending on the elderly was $615 billion, or $17,700 per person. For children, it was $148 billion or $2,100 per person.[12] Since 2000, the gap has widened, partly because of cuts to children's programs, but mostly because of continued huge increases in entitlement spending for the elderly.

It's been decades since child poverty was a matter of national debate. Franklin Roosevelt first made the case in the 1930's, when he successfully pushed for a wide variety of children's programs, including survivor's benefits for widows with children. Right through the early 1970's, presidential candidates of both parties—Hubert Humphrey, George McGovern, Richard Nixon—advanced the idea of European-style monthly income supplements to families with children. The cost of the Vietnam War put an end to the idea. Since then, the rise of conservatives that began in the 1980 election pushed aside serious discussion about reducing child poverty.

With 12.9 million children living below the poverty line and another 15.7 million in low-income families according to the latest data, it is way past time for childhood poverty to once again become an issue of political debate.[13]

Conservative Policy At Work

Chart 5.3 [14]

	Clinton Presidency Ends	Anti-government, Anti-tax Policies Take Effect				
	2000	**2001**	**2002**	**2003**	**2004**	**2005**
Income of Poorest 20% of Households	$11,514	$11,178	$10,845	$10,608	$10,587	$10,655
Families in Poverty	6,400,000	6,813,000	7,229,000	7,607,000	7,835,000	7,657,000
Uninsured People	39,804,000	41,207,000	43,574,000	44,961,000	45,306,000	46,577,000

According to U.S. government data, since the 2000 election income has dropped, poverty has increased, and health coverage has declined, as seen in Chart 5.3.

In the years after World War II, prolonged economic growth and low unemployment lifted many Americans out of poverty. The overall poverty rate fell throughout the 1950's, but it wasn't until the mid-1960's that policy makers concluded economic growth by itself would not be enough to eliminate poverty.

"We cannot and need not wait for the gradual growth of the economy to lift this forgotten fifth of our nation above the poverty line. We know what must be done, and this nation of abundance can surely afford to do it. Today, as in the past, higher employment and speedier economic growth are the cornerstones of a concerted attack on poverty—but general prosperity and growth leave untouched many of the roots of human poverty."
-Lyndon Johnson, 1964 Economic Report of the President. [15]

President Johnson's War on Poverty established many new programs to assist the poor: Medicare and Medicaid, Head Start, food stamps, low income energy assistance. Social Security benefits were indexed to account for inflation, and Supplemental Security Income was passed to give another helping hand to the elderly poor. As a result, the overall poverty rate declined, reaching a low of 11.1 percent in 1973— the lowest ever recorded. [16] Child poverty declined sharply too, hovering at a record low 15 percent in the late 1960's and early 1970's. Then in the 1980's, conservatives pushed through the first big cuts in social programs, arguing that private sector growth rather than government spending would do more to benefit the poor. They were wrong: even as the economy

Poverty and wealth

Chart 5.4

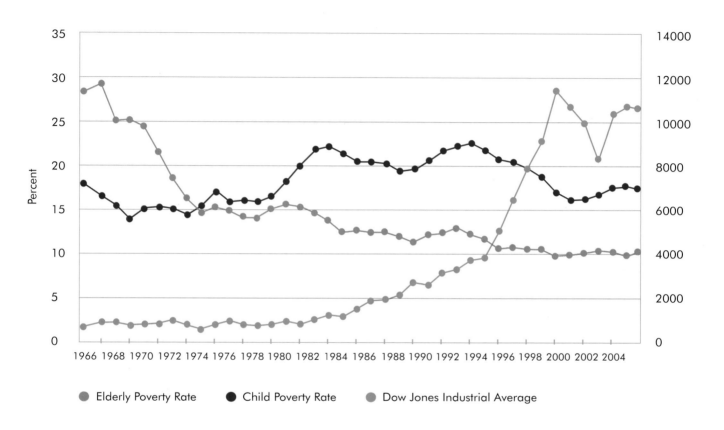

● Elderly Poverty Rate ● Child Poverty Rate ● Dow Jones Industrial Average

boomed in the 1980's the child poverty rate shot up once again, cresting at 22.7 percent in 1993. (Chart 5.4)

After taking office, President Clinton imposed new taxes, cut the federal deficit, and boosted spending on social programs. Predictably, the child poverty rate dropped back, reaching 16.3 percent in 2000.

Since 2001, the child poverty rate has increased by nearly 8 percent and now stands at 17.6 percent.[18]

Millions of additional children, while above the poverty line, live in low-income families—those earning less than $36,800, the minimum amount estimated for a family of four to be self-sufficient.[19] To earn that minimum, two parents need to work full-time at nine-dollar-an-hour jobs. That's almost twice as high as the current minimum wage of $5.15. There are now two million U.S. wage earners, with seven million dependent children, who make minimum wage or less.[20]

Conservative politicians have blocked any increase in the minimum wage since 1997. Adjusted for inflation, the minimum wage today would need to equal $6.31 in order to have the same purchasing power as it did in 1997.[21] Put another way, a worker earning today's minimum wage would have to work nine more hours every week to make up for her lost purchasing power.

How does that compare with Congressional wages? (Chart 5.5) Since 1997, Congress has treated itself to a nearly $32,000 annual pay raise accumulating $147,400 in new family income over the period. Minimum wage earners accumulated zero dollars in new family income. Are members of Congress working more hours? Spending more

Minimum Wage vs. Congressional Salaries

Chart 5.5[22]

Year	Annual Wage at Minimum Wage	Total New Family Income Over Base Year	Annual Salary of Members of Congress	Total New Family Income Over Base Year
1997	$10,712	$0	$133,600	$0
1998	$10,712	$0	$136,700	$3,100
1999	$10,712	$0	$136,700	$3,100
2000	$10,712	$0	$141,300	$7,700
2001	$10,712	$0	$145,100	$11,500
2002	$10,712	$0	$150,000	$16,400
2003	$10,712	$0	$154,700	$21,000
2004	$10,712	$0	$158,100	$24,500
2005	$10,712	$0	$162,100	$25,500
2006	$10,712	$0	$165,200	$31,600
10 Year Total	**$107,120**	**$0**	**$1,483,500**	**$147,400**

time with their constituents back home? Finding out what taxpayers want and need? If a 24 percent increase in pay was good enough for the political elite, shouldn't it have been good enough for the lowest paid and the least powerful? Conservative lawmakers were out of touch with the public on this issue: in a recent Pew Research Center poll, 83 percent of Americans said they support a minimum wage increase of two dollars an hour.[23]

At the same time that conservatives slammed the door on low-wage earners, their tax policies contributed to extreme concentrations of wealth: one percent of Americans possess 32.7 percent of the nation's privately held assets while the bottom 50 percent controls 2.8 percent.[24] Wealth began to become super concentrated after the 2000 election, when conservatives finally gained control of both Congress and the White House.

The administration chose "compassionate conservatism" to address the nation's social ills. That's fine, but government partnerships with community and faith-based charities were hardly a new idea. In every state, such groups already play an indispensable role in assisting children and families. When I served as Maine's human services commissioner, we contracted with hundreds of charitable organizations to deliver a wide array of health and social services. Everyone I know, liberal, moderate, and conservative alike, agrees this approach is a good one. So what's the problem? Compassionate conservatism went awry when it became a rationale to cut services to children and families. As helpful as faith-based groups can be, they are no substitute for federal anti-poverty programs. I've talked with large foundations and small churches, and all agree: the magnitude of our poverty problem requires *more* government intervention, not less. There simply are not sufficient private charitable dollars to cover legitimate public social needs—not in the other rich democracies, and not in the United States.

When George Bush served as governor of Texas, the epicenter of compassionate conservatism, how effective was it in alleviating poverty among low-income Texans? Here is how Texas ranks nationally:[25]

- 1st in the percentage of uninsured children

- 1st in food insecurity

- 2nd in the percentage of the population that goes hungry

- 2nd in teen pregnancy

- 5th in the overall poverty rate

- 47th in welfare and food stamps benefits paid to the needy

- 50th in the percentage of fully-immunized two-year-olds

These poor outcomes in Texas are the direct result of conservative principles. Yet the politicians who dream up the harsh policies that produce these poor outcomes refuse to acknowledge their failure, stubbornly insisting that yet more tax breaks and more cuts in programs for children are good for America.

If it could, the administration would impose Texas standards on the rest of the nation, as seen in its 2007 proposed budget:

- A 10 percent proposed cut in food stamps. One million participants would have lost benefits. Seventy percent of food stamp recipients are female, and over half are children.[26]

- A $2.5 billion cut in WIC (the special supplemental nutrition program for women, infants, and children) funding over five years. By 2011, WIC funding would have been 13 percent below the 2006 level, and 474,000 would have lost nutritional assistance.[27]

- Elimination of the Commodity Supplement Food Program. Millions of Americans would have gone hungry.[28]

- A 40% cut in the housing voucher program affecting 800,000 Americans.[29]

Although these measures failed in 2006, the administration and Congress passed a budget that cut Medicaid to children, weakened enforcement of court-ordered child support payments, and reduced child care assistance.

When President Lyndon Johnson first looked poverty in the face, he and his moderate and liberal allies in Congress pushed through programs that benefited millions of children and families. When conservatives saw the shameful state of U.S. poverty…they looked the other way.

Our children deserve better.

Impact of anti-government/anti-tax policy on poverty in Texas
Chart 5.6

	U.S. Average	Texas	Texas Rank
Percentage of Population under 18 living in poverty [30]	19%	25%	5
Percent of households experiencing food insecurity [31]	11.40%	16.40%	1
Maximum Aid Benefit Parent and 2 children [32]	$420	$201	48

Teen Births/TANF "welfare" payment rates

Top States vs. Bottom States • Chart 5.7

Rank	State	Births to teens 15-19 per 1000 girls 2003 [33]	Maximum Monthly TANF Benefit for a family of 3, January 2003 [34]
1	New Hampshire	18.2	$625.00
2	Vermont	18.9	$709.00
3	Massachusetts	23.0	$618.00
4	Connecticut	24.8	$636.00
5	Maine	24.9	$485.00
6	New Jersey	25.5	$424.00
7	Minnesota	26.6	$532.00
8	North Dakota	26.8	$477.00
9	New York	28.2	$577.00
10	Pennsylvania	31.2	$421.00
	Median Top 10	**25.2**	**$554.50**
41	Nevada	53.0	$348.00
42	Tennessee	53.5	$185.00
42	Georgia	53.5	$280.00
44	Oklahoma	55.9	$292.00
45	Louisiana	56.0	$240.00
46	Arkansas	59.0	$204.00
47	Arizona	61.1	$347.00
48	Mississippi	62.5	$170.00
49	New Mexico	62.7	$389.00
50	Texas	62.9	$201.00
	Median Bottom 10	**57.5**	**$260.00**

So much for conservative dogma that higher welfare payments encourage more out of wedlock births: Teens in the bottom 10 states give birth at a rate twice as high as teens in the top 10—even though welfare payments are less than half of those in the top 10. Teen girls in Texas are 3 times more likely to give birth than teens in New Hampshire—even though welfare benefits in New Hampshire are triple those of Texas.

Child Poverty

Top States vs. Bottom States • Chart 5.8 [35]

Rank	State	Child Poverty Rate
1	New Hampshire	9%
2	Utah	11%
2	Wyoming	11%
2	Maryland	11%
5	New Jersey	12%
5	Connecticut	12%
5	Minnesota	12%
8	Virginia	13%
8	Hawaii	13%
8	North Dakota	13%
Median Top 10		**12%**
41	Kentucky	22%
42	Oklahoma	23%
42	South Carolina	23%
44	Texas	25%
44	Alabama	25%
44	Arkansas	25%
47	West Virginia	26%
47	New Mexico	26%
49	Louisiana	28%
50	Mississippi	31%
Median Bottom 10		**25%**

A child in the bottom ten states is more than twice as likely to be living in poverty as a child in the top ten states. A child in Mississippi is more than three times as likely to live in poverty as a child in New Hampshire.

The Impact of Taxes and Transfers on Child Poverty Across the States

Top States vs. Bottom States • Chart 5.9 [36]

Rank	State	% of children in poverty—state	County with highest child poverty rate 1999	% of children in poverty—county
1	New Hampshire	9.7	Coos County	11.9
2	Connecticut	10.5	New Haven County	13.3
3	Delaware	13.8	Sussex County	15.3
4	Vermont	11.7	Orleans County	19.0
5	Hawaii	14.4	Hawaii County	21.7
6	Nevada	18.8	Mineral County	21.9
7	Iowa	12.4	Page County	22.3
8	Minnesota	10.7	Beltrami County	22.4
8	New Jersey	11.8	Hudson County	22.4
10	Rhode Island	21.0	Providence County	22.7
	Median Top 10	**12.1**		**21.8**
41	Arkansas	25.9	Phillips County	45.6
42	New Mexico	27.7	Luna County	47.1
43	South Carolina	22.8	Allendale County	48.1
44	Alabama	23.3	Perry County	49.2
45	Mississippi	31.0	Holmes County	52.4
46	West Virginia	24.4	McDowell County	53.0
47	Kentucky	25.0	Owsley County	56.4
48	Louisiana	30.0	East Carroll Parish	56.8
49	Texas	22.9	Starr County	59.5
50	South Dakota	14.8	Buffalo County	61.8
	Median Bottom 10	**24.7**		**52.7**

This chart explains a lot about why child poverty varies so much from state to state. Not only do the top 10 states have child poverty rates just half that of the bottom states, they also adopt policies that limit how much the child poverty rate can climb in any one county—typically 10 percentage points or fewer. In contrast, the child poverty gap within bottom states is 20 to 45 percentage points.

6. TAXES AND GOVERNMENT
ARE NOT FOUR LETTER WORDS

"What did President Roosevelt's New Deal mean for your family," I asked my great-uncle Ralph, who was a child during the Great Depression of the 1930's. "Well," he said, "before FDR, Dad drove a truck for a meat-packing company, delivering and unloading beef 10 to 12 hours a day, six days a week, and he felt lucky to have the job. He went to bed exhausted as soon as he got home Saturday, and on Sunday he spent most of the day in bed. But after FDR got some new law passed, Dad had the same job, but he had to work only 40 hours a week, and he got the same pay! On Saturdays he started taking us fishing, and on Sundays Mother made it clear he no longer had an excuse to not attend church..."

Uncle Ralph's family and millions more benefited forever from the wise application of federal power and policy.

The major advances in health and well-being that our country experienced in the 20th century were the direct result of federal tax support for medical research, hospitals, maternal and child health services, higher education for doctors and nurses, and public health measures such as clean drinking water and city-wide sanitation systems. Thanks to long-term voter support for such tax expenditures, that is, investments in ourselves, steady progress has been made for decades in health, education, and social indicators for children.

Today, those gains are put at risk of being reversed thanks to the two myths that have underpinned conservative ideology: first, that the federal government can't do anything right and works against the public's interest; and second, that to collect taxes is akin to outright thievery. Wrapped in simple-minded slogans like, "It's your money; you know best how to spend it," and "We're from the government and are here to help you," these myths enabled conservatives to capture the White House and Congress. But they were a great disservice to the nation and harmed our children.

Vote With Your Feet
Conservatives said states, being "closer
to the people," are more suited to deliver
programs. And when states aren't responsive?
Citizens could "vote with their feet," moving to
a state which would "compete" to serve them.
But how does an eight-year-old in a wheelchair,
whose parents are in prison, vote with his feet?

In contrast, the social programs pushed through by Presidents Roosevelt, Truman, and Johnson, in particular, alleviated widespread poverty among the elderly and were instrumental in creating the nation's great middle class. The actions of these progressive leaders helped enact civil rights laws to end discrimination, provided pensions and health care for tens of millions, sent GI's to college after WWII, and allowed millions of citizens to buy their first homes. For decades, federal laws were enacted to make the workplace safer, control predatory lending, give disadvantaged children a head start, eradicate most of the major communicable diseases, and alleviate hunger. The federal government financed these programs mainly with balanced budgets paid for by taxes that were levied based on a citizen's ability to pay.

To this day, these programs and policies provide the stability essential for democracy and capitalism to work in tandem, and to create the profits that fuel our economy. Federal investments and regulations have contributed to an unparalleled political and economic climate found nowhere else. They have fostered the creation of vast wealth that benefits all social and economic groups, children included.

For the past 25 years, conservative lawmakers worked to undo the federal formula that helped to create these advances. What has it gotten us? The federal budget is awash in red ink. Federal regulatory agencies have been weakened. The IRS has far less capacity to audit wealthy taxpayers and indeed, low-income wage earners are far more likely to be questioned by IRS investigators.[1] Wealth is more concentrated than ever before. Progressive taxes have been cut and replaced by regressive payroll, lottery, casino, and property taxes. The estate tax, meant to regulate inherited fortunes from one generation to the next, is in jeopardy. The conservative agenda to slash federal revenues inevitably meant fewer investments in children.

Although this generation of conservative members of Congress voted for sharp cuts in federal children's health and social programs, in previous decades a broad coalition of moderates and liberals worked together to expand them. I estimate that federal funds still provide 50 percent to 80 percent of state spending on child health, nutrition, income assistance, and social services. The exact amount of federal funds is based on formulas which channel more aid to poorer states, the idea being to create a floor below which no child falls. As seen in Chart 6.1, the richer states that contribute more in federal taxes are typically blue and mostly from the north, while the states that receive more federal tax revenues than they pay are typically red and from the south.

One of the chief architects of compassionate conservatism, a staunch supporter of cuts in children's programs, has boasted, "I don't want to abolish government. I simply want to reduce it to the size where I can drag it into the bathroom and drown it in the bathtub."[2] Which federal program would he "drown?" The Supplemental Security Income program, which serves five million children whose parents have died or become disabled? Or the Medicaid program, which provides basic health care to millions of children? Or the Maternal and Child Health program, which has kept our infant and maternal mortality rates low? How about the program that serves mentally retarded children, the one that provides child care for working parents, or the child protection program that tries to heal five-year-olds who have been sexually abused?

Federal Redistributive Policy at Work in the States

Top States vs. Bottom States • Chart 6.1[3]

Rank	State	Federal Spending per $1.00 paid in Federal Taxes
1	New Jersey	$0.57
2	New Hampshire	$0.64
3	Connecticut	$0.65
4	Minnesota	$0.70
4	Nevada	$0.70
6	Illinois	$0.73
7	Massachusetts	$0.78
7	California	$0.78
9	New York	$0.80
9	Colorado	$0.80
	Median Top 10	**$0.72**
41	Kentucky	$1.52
42	Hawaii	$1.58
42	Virginia	$1.58
44	Montana	$1.60
45	Alabama	$1.69
46	North Dakota	$1.75
47	West Virginia	$1.82
48	Mississippi	$1.83
49	Alaska	$1.89
50	New Mexico	$1.99
	Median Bottom 10	**$1.72**

The bottom 10 states receive more than double the federal support that goes to the top 10. New Mexico receives nearly four times more than New Jersey from the national treasury.

Just how much federal funding goes to state programs for children?

- Medicaid provided health care for 19.7 million children in 2005.[4] In fiscal year 2005, it is estimated the federal government provided $174 billion for Medicaid.[5]

- The federal State Children's Insurance Program helps provide health care to more than four million low-income children not eligible for Medicaid. The federal share was $3.12 billion in fiscal year 2004.[6]

- In fiscal year 2004, nationwide funding for the prevention and treatment of child abuse and neglect totaled roughly $23 billion, including $11.6 billion in federal funds.[7]

- In fiscal year 2004, child care assistance included $8.08 billion in federal funds.[8]

- In 2003, the federal government spent $6.7 billion for Head Start, serving approximately 909,600 pre-kindergartners.[9]

- In the 2003-2004 school year, the federal government funded the School Lunch Program with $6.5 billion, feeding more than 28 million kids each day.[10]

- In 2005, the Women, Infants, and Children program served more than eight million people; spending totaled about $3.6 billion.[11]

- The Food Stamp program provides benefits to 25.6 million people (12.8 million children), at a cost of $31 billion.[12]

- The Earned Income Tax Credit serves 19.2 million families at a cost of $34.4 billion,[13] lifting 2.4 million children out of poverty in the process.[14]

These federal programs are typically administered by state and local governments, with extensive contracting through the non-profit sector, including faith-based organizations. The federal taxes that fund these programs have strengthened families, made kids healthier, and boosted the U.S. economy.

Polls Show Voters Want More Investments in Their Children and Grandchildren—Even Over Tax Cuts

In a recent national survey voters preferred investments over more tax breaks by 68%-24%.

Child Investments Preferred to Tax/Budget Cuts

Chart 6.2 [15]

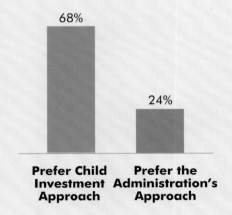

Some people believed that compassionate conservatism could better serve the interests of distressed children than the federal government. But exactly how would such a vague concept protect a three-year-old who is sexually abused, or assist a severely disabled bed-bound child, or a lonely teenager considering suicide? Certainly, we want churches to help and foundations to step forward. Yes, neighbors should be kind, volunteers are angels, and corporations should contribute more to United Way. It sounds good, but it just doesn't add up to enough. When I worked for a terrific United Way in Maine before becoming the state's human services commissioner, I discovered that all of the United Way organizations in Maine raised funds equal to just one percent of the department of human services' budget. If everyone had doubled their giving, it would have equaled two percent. The simple fact is that the number of people who need a helping hand is much too big to be handled by private organizations alone.

Voters know that special interests have dominated Congress. In one national poll, 63 percent said children's needs are routinely shoved aside by stronger groups. Just 24 percent think Congress does enough to help working families with children.[16] And they're right. Since 2001, conservatives have granted tax breaks in the trillions to special interests. The subsequent loss in federal revenue virtually assures additional reductions in spending on children for years to come:

- Projected federal revenue loss for 2001-2013 caused by the 2001, 2002, and 2003 tax cuts is $1.7 trillion. Additionally, if other temporary cuts are made permanent, revenue loss climbs to $3.6 trillion. When interest payments are added due to higher debt, the lost revenues exceed $4 trillion.[17]

- Congress's recent tax breaks raised the child tax credit to $1,000, but it left out millions of working families with children who will receive no tax credit whatsoever. And because the fiscal year 2004 Budget Resolution cuts domestic spending $167.7 billion over 10 years, low-wage families who depend on federal income supplements will be hardest hit.[18]

- While these anticipated cuts in domestic spending surely will harm many children, they are relatively modest when compared to total federal spending on children. More ominous are future deep tax breaks, already adopted, which promise sharp cuts in Head Start, after-school, mental health, sexual abuse treatment, and other children's programs. The result? More hurt children and a less productive workforce to support an aging population.

This is ridiculous. The evidence is overwhelming that smart investments in children save money:

- The High/Scope Foundation's Perry Preschool program saved $150,000 per participant in crime costs alone. The project produced a net savings of $7.16—including more than six dollars in crime savings—for every dollar invested.[19]

- The Quantum Opportunities after-school program produced $3 in benefits for every $1 spent, even without counting the savings realized from the sharp drop in crime committed by boys in the program.[20]

- For each high-risk youth prevented from adopting a life of crime, the country would save $1.7 million.[21]

- Prevent Child Abuse America estimates that child abuse and neglect costs Americans $94 billion a year, with two-thirds of that cost due to crime.[22]

Volumes of research confirm what we all know intuitively: early attention to the needs of children by parents and communities is the best way to ensure productive and emotionally healthy young adults. Visit www.everychildmatters.org for links to many sites presenting research on the effectiveness of programs.

The federal government has been a key player in supporting research about healthy child development, and that's exactly what it should be doing. It's our government; members of Congress and the president serve at the will of voters, and we care about our kids. Most people agree that the federal government should do more, not less, to help families. The question isn't whether to help, but how to help and how to pay for it.

No one I know thinks the federal government should deliver services directly to children and families. Services are best delivered by non-profit organizations with local boards of directors, by church groups, and by local, county, and state governments. The proper role of the federal government is to create national performance standards, provide oversight and evaluation, and supply most of the cash via progressive personal and corporate income taxes and estate taxes. A leadership role by the national government is essential: whether children and families are successful should not be an accident of geography, dependent upon the state where they were born or live.

But now, just at the moment when the country is experiencing a huge investment gap in its children, we find the national treasury is bare. While the Iraq war and Hurricane Katrina have contributed, declining federal revenue is overwhelmingly due to the trillions in tax breaks. The next chart says it all about the deteriorating U.S. budget situation.

Balanced Budgets: Tax and Spend Ideology vs. Don't Tax but Still Spend Ideology

Chart 6.4 [23]

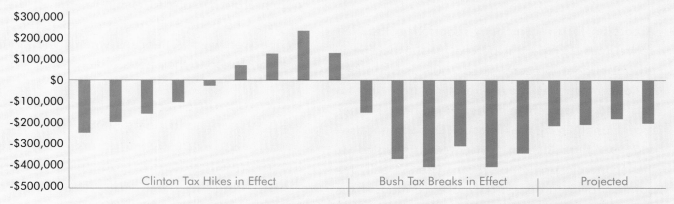

Clinton Tax Hikes in Effect   Bush Tax Breaks in Effect   Projected

1993 1994 1995 1996 1997 1998 1999 2000 2001 2002 2003 2004 2005 2006 2007 2008 2009 2010 2011

■ Budget surplus/deficit (-) (millions of dollars)

When conservatives took full control of the government in 2001, the non-partisan Congressional Budget Office projected federal budget surpluses for 2002-2011 totaling $5.6 trillion. In a complete switch, the CBO now estimates that instead of a surplus there will be a deficit of $2.7 trillion, a reversal of $8.3 trillion!

According to a recent study reported in the New York Times, "Fifty-eight percent of the decline in official budget forecasts since 2001 [is attributed] to lower revenues mainly resulting from the tax cuts, and 42 percent to higher spending."[24] Further, recent analysis by the Treasury Department itself suggests that the tax cuts were unrelated to the economic upturn of recent years.[25] Still, the administration proposes to make permanent the tax breaks enacted since 2001. The lost revenue will be three times larger than the projected Social Security shortfall over the next 75 years.

We now know conclusively that fiscally reckless tax breaks have made the United States the world's largest debtor nation, saddled future generations with huge debt, and threatened whatever hope we have to close the investment gap in children's programs. Quite a record.

Unfortunately, it continues. For example, in Chapter Three, we documented the widespread existence of child abuse in the United States. Even official government reports show that many state child welfare agencies are severely under-funded and can't deal effectively with the problem. On the same page of this morning's paper I'm looking at two seemingly unrelated articles that actually are very much connected. The first describes terrible suffering in families with severe child abuse, including the permanent separation of children from their families.[26] The second reports that the administration plans to eliminate half of the IRS lawyers who handle gift and estate tax returns filed by the wealthiest Americans when their fortunes are transferred to their heirs.[27]

Did conservatives lose their senses? Children were suffering and being removed from their own homes because their parents couldn't get the treatment needed to stop child abuse, and the government responded by taking yet more tax money off the table to support the lifestyles of the super rich. Is this the kind of government policy we want?

With so many children needing help, why would we want to eliminate the estate tax? Is there a fairer tax than one which claims a portion of huge estates, sometimes valued in the billions, that are passed on to heirs who have done nothing to earn the money except to 'choose' the right parents?

If we are going to invest in children's programs, we have to pay for them. Politicians can say what they want, but except for cuts in programs that serve politically defenseless poor people, the federal budget is rapidly expanding, not shrinking. Conservatives could have brought the budget under control with a combination of cuts in entitlement programs and tax increases, but they were unwilling to take such strong medicine. For decades, they accused liberals of over-taxing American citizens and businesses, and spending too much on federal programs. But which was more responsible: the tax and spend policies of the Clinton years, which left the government with a huge budget surplus, or the don't-tax-but-still-spend policies put in place by conservatives since 2001, which left the budget awash in red ink and our country dependent on foreign creditors?

Here's what Warren Buffet, the world's second richest man, who opposes repeal of the estate tax, thinks about inherited wealth:

"Certainly neither Susie nor I ever thought we should pass huge amounts of money along to our children. Our kids are great. But I would argue that when your kids have all the advantages anyway, in terms of how they grow up and the opportunities they have for education, including what they learn at home—I would say it's neither right nor rational to be flooding them with money. In effect, they've had a giant head start in a society that aspires to be a meritocracy. Dynastic mega-wealth would further tilt the playing field that we ought to be trying instead to level."[28]

The conservative tax breaks overwhelmingly benefit high-income households. In 2005:[29]

- The bottom one-fifth of households received an average combined tax break of $18, raising their after-tax income by 0.3 percent.

- Households with incomes over $1 million received an average tax break of $103,000, an increase of 5.4 percent in their after-tax income.

- 97 percent of the 2001 tax breaks for the rich that are still being phased in will go to households with incomes above $200,000.

Here's how the conservative Speaker of the House in 2006 justified the unequal distribution of these tax breaks: "Well folks, if you earn $40,000 a year and have a family of two, you don't pay any taxes. So you probably, if you don't pay any taxes, you are not going to get a big tax cut."[30]

Apparently the Speaker would be surprised to learn that lower income families pay the highest proportion of income in taxes when all forms of taxes are considered. Does he know that regressive payroll taxes automatically deducted from the paychecks of working Americans total $72.2 billion more a year than is paid out in Social Security? And does he know that the surplus is used to run general government operations?[31] What about property taxes and gas taxes? Maybe if the Speaker knew more about these taxes, he'd be more sympathetic to middle class families. But maybe not.

Income inequality has been increasing in the United States since 1979 and shows no sign of slowing under the newest tax proposals. The richest one percent of households (people earning more than $1 million annually) now get a larger share, 16.77 percent, of national income than at any time since 1937, with the exception of the years 1997-2001, during the extraordinary stock market boom.[32]

The president repeatedly states that his tax cuts are strengthening the U.S. economy, but the facts do not support his claim. Every recession in U.S. history has been followed by a period of economic growth, whether taxes were lowered, raised, or remained stable. But let's suppose that the administration is right, that tax cuts do help boost the economy. Even if that's true, why would you provide tax breaks to the super rich instead of to poor and middle class wage earners?

If conservatives really wanted to use tax breaks to increase economic growth, they would have given a payroll tax break to millions of Americans who would have spent the funds on consumer goods and improved business earnings in the process. Instead, they gave more tax breaks to the rich. How did they pay for these tax breaks? According to Citizens for Tax Justice, they "are being paid for entirely with borrowed money. In fact, over the fiscal 2002-07 period, the national debt, including amounts owed to the Social Security Trust Fund, will balloon by $3 trillion. The cost of this borrowing binge will ultimately come out of taxpayers' pockets, either through spending cuts or future tax hikes."[33] In the short term, the government borrowed more money through the sale of treasury notes. Who buys these risk-free notes? Well-off Americans buy them, using the tax breaks they just received from Congress! The net effect of all of this borrowing and spending can be seen in Chart 6.5, which shows that 99% of taxpayers are net losers from the 2001-06 tax cuts.

Average Tax Cuts and Added Federal Debt,
by Income Group in 2001-2006, per family member
Chart 6.5 [34]

Income Group (Average Annual Income)	Average Tax Cut per person	Average New Debt per person	Net Gain or (Loss) per person
Lowest 20% ($11,200)	$299	$7,468	($7,169)
Second 20% ($22,900)	$1,244	$8,132	($6,888)
Middle 20% ($37,500)	$1,855	$8,936	($7,081)
Fourth 20% ($61,800)	$2,580	$9,996	($7,416)
Next 15% ($107,000)	$4,576	$11,620	($7,044)
Next 4% ($230,000)	$9,771	$16,280	($6,509)
Top 1% ($1,272,000)	$84,482	$54,130	$30,352

There's something else we ought to consider about the federal income tax. It was no small feat in the first place to adopt the progressive income tax. It should not be surrendered to today's fiscally reckless conservatives without a fight. The progressive tax was first introduced to capture some of the wealth created by robber barons during the Civil War. It was bitterly opposed by the rich when it was permanently adopted in 1894, but the following year, in 1895, the Supreme Court declared the tax unconstitutional. It took another 18 years to restore it, via adoption of the Sixteenth Amendment in 1913.[35] Earlier generations of Americans clearly understood that progressive taxes are essential to democracy and its commitment to equal opportunity for all children.

The current generation of anti-government, anti-tax conservatives seems determined to prove our ancestors wrong.

Our children deserve much better.

Tax Revenue and Expenditures in Texas

Chart 6.5

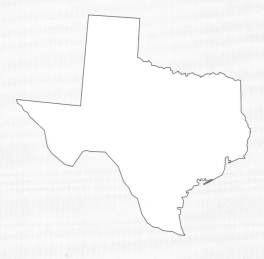

	U.S. Average	Texas	Texas Rank
Per Capita Tax Revenue raised [36]	$2,025.98	$1,368.45	50
Per Capita Total General Expenditures [37]	$4,797.08	$3,441.53	50

Texas's generally poor indicators for children are directly related to its unwillingness to tax itself. Last in revenue raised, it is 33rd in per capita income.

Taxes in the Rich Democracies

Chart 6.6

Except for paying slightly more in taxes than the Japanese, Americans pay far less in taxes than the other rich democracies. Put differently, we Americans make far fewer public investments in our children and families, as seen in poorer outcome indicators found throughout this book.

% of gross earnings given up in tax, average income family of four [38]	G7 Countries	Total taxation as % of GDP [39]
39.4%	France	45.3%
35.6%	Italy	42.0%
32.6%	Germany	37.9%
17.8%	UK	37.4%
20.5%	Canada	35.8%
19.4%	US	29.6%
20.4%	Japan	27.1%

Per Capita Income

Top States vs. Bottom States • Chart 6.7 [40]

Rank	State	Per Capita Income	Tax Burden Rank
1	Connecticut	$51,390.77	1
2	New Jersey	$47,819.42	3
3	Massachusetts	$47,047.45	4
4	Maryland	$43,602.57	15
5	New York	$43,119.06	2
6	New Hampshire	$41,258.35	34
7	Minnesota	$41,158.14	11
8	Illinois	$39,948.23	16
9	Washington	$39,768.43	8
10	California	$39,715.04	9
	Median Top 10	**$42,188.71**	
41	Alabama	$30,576.07	49
42	South Carolina	$30,536.46	39
43	Oklahoma	$30,435.00	44
44	Montana	$30,432.96	41
45	Idaho	$30,231.35	42
46	New Mexico	$29,136.93	18
47	Utah	$28,766.82	25
48	West Virginia	$28,540.72	38
49	Arkansas	$28,442.62	33
50	Mississippi	$27,404.64	46
	Median Bottom 10	**$29,684.14**	

Per capita income in the bottom 10 states is less than three-quarters of per capita income in the top 10 states. People in Mississippi earn slightly more than half what their counterparts in Connecticut earn. Why is that? What does Connecticut do differently than Mississippi? Connecticut—and the other top states—generally make greater long-term investments in their children's health, education, and social welfare...and long-term benefits can be seen in the higher incomes their citizens earn.

The Relationship of Tax Burden to Overall Child Well-Being

Top States vs. Bottom States • Chart 6.8 [41]

Rank	State	Total Tax Burden	Overall Child Well-being Rank
1	Connecticut	33.5%	3
2	New York	32.6%	22
3	New Jersey	31.4%	7
4	Massachusetts	31.1%	10
4	Wyoming	31.1%	28
6	Maine	30.8%	11
7	Rhode Island	30.7%	31
8	Washington	30.1%	17
9	California	29.9%	18
10	Wisconsin	29.8%	13
	Median Top 10	**30.9%**	**15**
41	Montana	27.0%	34
42	Idaho	26.9%	20
43	Louisiana	26.8%	49
44	Oklahoma	26.5%	40
45	North Dakota	26.4%	9
45	Mississippi	26.4%	50
47	South Dakota	26.3%	14
48	Tennessee	26.1%	46
49	Alabama	25.7%	43
50	Alaska	25.0%	35
	Median Bottom 10	**26.4%**	**37.5**

This chart shows clearly that states that tax themselves at a higher rate—that is, they make more investments in their citizens—produce decidedly better outcomes for their children. The self-imposed 17% higher total tax burden in the top 10 states produces a high return on their investments.

7. MAKING NEW INVESTMENTS
IN CHILDREN A NATIONAL POLITICAL PRIORITY

Americans want more investments in their children and grandchildren. First, to improve each child's life chances for success, but also because they know the nation's global competitiveness depends on it and an aging population requires it.

I have identified the broad major investments that are needed over the next decade. I have not prescribed specific solutions because there is no one best way to construct the investment. That is something that needs to be debated and determined by our elected leaders.

The good news is that we know a lot about healthy human growth and development. A vast amount of research exists that demonstrates the effectiveness of various policies and clinical interventions, links to some of which can be found at www.everychildmatters.org.

With respect to the money needed to make new investments in children, youth and families, the U.S. remains a wealthy country which can easily afford the cost. A few suggestions on where to find the necessary funds are listed elsewhere in this chapter. The return on such an investment would be huge and would benefit all Americans. In all instances of new investments, I support universal access to the programs created as long as they are provided on a sliding scale, fee-for-service based on the ability to pay. That is, those families using services who have the lowest incomes would pay little or nothing, and those with the highest incomes would pay for all or most of the services they use. (The exception is health insurance; no sliding-scale fee would apply. Everyone would be fully insured.) Services should meet national standards and there should be rigorous evaluations to ensure program effectiveness.

10 YEAR, $500 BILLION INVEST
IN KIDS AGENDA

Child Abuse and Neglect

The Challenge
There are three million reports of child abuse and neglect a year. Thousands of children are killed and severely injured, leaving life-long harmful consequences for individual children and the families and communities they live in.

The Investment
Fully fund the wide array of proven prevention and treatment programs which together can sharply reduce child abuse and neglect while strengthening families.

The Benefits
Less violence, crime, poverty, educational failure, unemployment, imprisonment. High financial return on investments.

Child Health

The Challenge
Nine million children are without health insurance. Millions are not receiving timely or comprehensive medical attention, allowing preventable illness to strike them.

The Investment
Provide coverage to all uninsured children guaranteeing uninterrupted care for every child.

The Benefits
Healthier children and lower health costs.

Early Childhood Education

The Challenge
Millions of pre-school children are unable to take advantage of early learning opportunities proven to improve school readiness.

The Investment
Fully fund Early Head Start services for infants and toddlers in poverty and make available quality preschool education for all children.

The Benefits
Improved school performance, reductions in crime and acquisition of skills to become contributing citizens. Proven high return on investment.

Child Care

The Challenge
Affordable, high quality care is unavailable to millions of children with working parents.

The Investment
Make quality child care—including infant and toddler care—affordable for all working families.

The Benefits
Safe, nurturing and stimulating conditions for children. Improved school readiness. Increased job productivity by parents.

Mental Health

The Challenge
Millions of young children and youth experience early emotional problems which are serious enough to impede learning and healthy development.

The Investment
Provide a full array of training, prevention and treatment services allowing parents and providers of care to children to intervene early.

The Benefits
Emotionally healthy children, youth and young adults—the key to creating a productive and emotionally satisfying adulthood.

After-School Programs

The Challenge
Millions of children and youth who are in unsupervised situations at the end of each school day would benefit from participation in quality after-school programs.

The Investment
Make available high quality after–school programs to all children and youth.

The Benefits
Improved school performance, less crime, safer children.

Poverty and Working Families

The Challenge
More than 12 million children and youth live below the poverty line. Millions more are in low wage families who work full time, but simply cannot earn enough to provide for basic family needs.

The Investment
A combination of tax credits and deductions, minimum wage increases, family allowances, subsidized health insurance and child care, which guarantees that full-time, low wage workers receive a household income that does not fall below the federal poverty level.

The Benefits
Low poverty rates are associated with improved school performance, lower child abuse rates, less crime and domestic violence, safer housing, healthier lifestyles, less substance abuse, lower prison rates and numerous other indicators of child and adult well-being.

The vast majority of Americans support the principle that government has a moral responsibility to help provide for the health, education, and safety of children. Who doesn't believe in strengthening families? The healthy development of children fosters emotionally healthy young adults who can support our aging population and enable the United States to remain competitive in a global economy.

We may all agree with these goals, but that's not the direction in which the country has been heading. It's going to take a lot of time and money to meet these objectives. Yes, we remain a fabulous country, albeit a flawed one. But for decades we've avoided the major new social investments required for our families and our culture to thrive.

It's time for a renewed debate in Congress on the best ways our government and our culture can help families and children. The list below outlines the broad budget, political, and policy actions which I believe are needed to make the United States the greatest place in the world for children and families. I have not gotten into the details—that's another book, and other people have already written in great detail about successful programs and investments. Here is what I propose:

1. National leaders should call upon the candidates for the White House and the Congress to present their plans for addressing the needs of the country's children and families. The leaders should represent a broad, bipartisan perspective and make their views known at the start of the federal election cycle in 2007. A similar call should be made in each state to gubernatorial and legislative candidates.

2. The presidential nominees of both parties in 2008 should propose a 10 year, $500 billion invest-in-kids agenda. This agenda should be presented to the public and should respond to the many problems facing families. A prosperous American future demands progress on excessive imprisonment, child abuse, health insurance, poverty, early childcare and learning, housing, substance abuse, and wage supports for low income workers. In particular, we need a family-friendly workplace environment that permits greater balance between the demands of work and family.

3. The next president should feature the invest-in-kids agenda in the new Administration's first budget in 2009. The $500 billion is not as large as it might sound. In the same period, the amount spent on the Medicare drug program for seniors will cost more than $700 billion.

4. The next president should re-establish the tradition of convening a White House Conference on Children, Youth, and Families begun by President Theodore Roosevelt in 1909. These conferences, held every 10 years, set priorities, encourage debate, and showcase the widest possible representation of views. In preparation for the national conference in 2010, governors should convene similar gatherings in their states in 2009.

5. The new Congress should repeal a portion of the trillions in tax breaks given to the wealthiest 1% of Americans since 2001. This would allow our wealthy country to pay for the invest-in-kids agenda.

6. Alternately, the IRS could enforce the existing federal tax code to pay for the entire invest-in-kids agenda. According to a July 2006 report of the U.S. Senate Permanent Investigations Subcommittee, the nation's wealthiest individuals evade as much as $70 billion in tax payments each year. Aided by tax lawyers, bankers, and accountants, their monumental cheating forces additional tax burdens on an unsuspecting middle class. If the $70 billion owed annually was collected, $50 billion could be invested in the nation's children and $20 billion could be used to reduce a runaway national debt.

7. **New investments in children and families should be guided by proven research, strict accountability, and national performance standards.** They should be administered by a partnership of federal, state, and local government agencies, and non-profit, community-based organizations. Progress should be reported to the public. Efficient management is essential for public confidence.

8. **The press should provide greater coverage of children's needs.** Much like the monthly and quarterly reporting on the economy, the public should be kept abreast of the numbers of children insured, high school dropout rates, child abuse deaths, and other key indicators.

9. **The press should publish the roll call votes that members of Congress cast on children's issues.** They should also report on major legislation before Congress that affects children.

10. **Parents and grandparents should be mobilized to vote for candidates based on their positions on children's issues.** Children can't vote, but all adults who care about them can. Almost all of the nation's 73.2 million children have parents and grandparents who can vote. Tens of millions attend child-serving sites every day where the millions of staff who serve them also can be enlisted to vote. A good way to ensure greater representation of children on Election Day is to conduct non-partisan voter registration drives and get out the vote campaigns at child-serving sites. (The only child-serving sites where voter registration is prohibited by federal law are Head Start locations. About two-thirds of children served by Head Start are Black or Latino.)

11. Former offenders should have their voting privileges restored upon release from prison. **Millions of children have parents who are barred from voting because of time served in prison. This disenfranchisement especially affects minority families due to their disproportionate rate of imprisonment. It also means that their children are less well-represented at the ballot box.**

12. Congress and the President should put forward a plan to insure every child. **No other policy could do so much to lift child well-being. Support for such a plan would be the simplest way to measure the commitment of individual lawmakers to children.**

13. AARP should take a leadership role in urging Congress to support a $500 billion invest-in-kids agenda. **Grandparents should wield their oversized political muscle on behalf of all children, especially since the distribution of national wealth is largely determined at the ballot box. AARP and seniors have a moral responsibility to assure that all age groups share in the nation's bounty. Our aging population has as much to benefit from new investments in children as children themselves.**

14. The minimum wage should be raised by at least $2 per hour. **Congress should index the minimum wage to its own pay increases. That would allow the minimum pay scale to rise automatically each year, in the same way Congress now handles its own pay. If it's good enough for Congress, it's good enough for our lowest wage earners.**

15. Anyone who works full-time should receive sufficient income to equal the federal poverty level. The other rich democracies operate from a belief that a market-driven economy cannot by itself ensure that workers and their families receive sufficient income to meet minimum federal living standards. They are able to keep their child poverty rates much lower than ours through budget and tax policies that redistribute income: higher tax deductions for dependents, for example, or supplements to family income such as full payments for child care or health insurance.

16. Progressive taxation should be the centerpiece of U.S. tax laws. Those who make more money should be taxed at a progressively higher rate. Personal and corporate income taxes, along with the estate tax, are the fairest ways to pay for the basic education, safety, and health of all children—something which benefits all Americans. At present, there simply is not enough federal revenue on the table. Alternately, Congress could find the money needed for children if it eliminated the widely documented waste rampant in federal price supports for agriculture or weapons development, to name just two areas. But conservatives have been unwilling to take these actions because they would have required a confrontation with the very powerful special interests that have dominated policy-making in the administration and Congress. Members of Congress and presidents are dependent upon these powerful interests for campaign contributions. Which brings me to what I believe is the single most important measure necessary to assure the long term well-being of children...indeed, of the country.

17. All federal elections should be publicly financed. The budget priorities of Congress are morally corrupt. They harm our children and families, and they do not reflect the will of the American public. The American public, starting with its children, is not fairly represented in Congress. The gender, racial, economic, educational, and social differences between Congress and the public it is meant to serve are enormous. That's why public financing of elections is needed. In a representative democracy, legitimate power is bestowed at the ballot box. But in a vast country of 300 million people that spans two oceans, winning public office is expensive. It is not uncommon for a single Senate race to cost tens of millions of dollars. Where does that money come from? From powerful special interests who want something from the Congress—licenses, less regulation, cash subsidies, tax breaks, contracts. In this environment the needs of children stand little chance. It would cost only a few billion dollars to publicly finance federal elections, thereby allowing anyone to seek high public office and ending dependency on powerful special interests to finance campaigns. Who do we want members of Congress to turn to for campaign contributions? Mining, oil, and tobacco interests? Defense, gambling, and pharmaceutical interests? Or American citizens? Which would be in the best interest of children?

We can do this. Our children are waiting.

Chapter 1: *We Can Do Better Than This*

Citations

1 Suicide and Homicide numbers from: Centers for Disease Control and Prevention, National Center for Injury Prevention and Control. Web-based Injury Statistics Query and Reporting System (WISQARS) [online]. (2005) [cited Sept. 20, 2006]. Available from URL: www.cdc.gov/ncipc/wisqars; Child Abuse and Neglect numbers from: U.S. Department of Health and Human Services, Administration on Children, Youth and Families. Child Maltreatment 2004 (Washington, DC: U.S. Government Printing Office, 2006).

2 Congressional Budget Office. Federal Spending on the Elderly and Children. Accessed at http://ftp.cbo.gov/showdoc.cfm?index=2300&sequence=0 on Sept. 20, 2006

3 Poverty data: DeNavas-Walt, Carmen, Bernadette D. Proctor, and Cheryl Hill Lee, U.S. Census Bureau, Current Population Reports, P60-231, Income, Poverty, and Health Insurance Coverage in the United States: 2005, Table B-2, p. 52, U.S. Government Printing Office, Washington, DC, 2006.; Dow Jones data: Accessed through a search at http://finance.yahoo.com/q/hp?s=%5EDJI Numbers represent value of the Dow Jones Industrial Average on the last day of the year. Accessed on September 20,2006

4 Mason-Dixon Polling and Research, 800 registered voters nationally conducted from February 19th to 27th, 2003.

5 American Heritage Dictionary of the English Language, Boston: Houghton Mifflin, 1967

6 American Heritage Dictionary of the English Language, Boston: Houghton Mifflin, 1967

7 Mason-Dixon Polling and Research, 400 registered voters in Texas Congressional District 17 conducted from November 3rd to 5th, 2004.
8 Tax Foundation, Total Income by State Per Capita, 2005, Accessed at http://www.taxfoundation.org/news/show/290.html on September 25, 2006

9 DeNavas-Walt, Carmen, Bernadette D. Proctor, and Cheryl Hill Lee, U.S. Census Bureau, Current Population Reports, P60-231, Income, Poverty, and Health Insurance Coverage in the United States: 2005, Table 10, p. 27, U.S. Government Printing Office, Washington, DC, 2006.

10 U.S. Department of Health and Human Services, Administration on Children, Youth and Families. Child Maltreatment 2004, Table 4-1, p. 68. (Washington, DC: U.S. Government Printing Office, 2006).

11 The Annie E. Casey Foundation, KIDS COUNT State Level Data Online, www.kidscount.org

Chapter 2: *Health Care for All Children*

Citations

1 Children's Defense Fund. Child Health Division. CHIP Toolkit, p. 2 Washington, DC: 1999 Accessed at http://www.childrensdefense.org/site/DocServer/healthtoolkit.pdf?docID=631 September 25, 2006

2 Families USA. One in Three: Non-Elderly Americans Without Health Insurance, 2002-2003. p. 16 (Washington, DC: Families USA, 2004)

3 Families USA. One in Three: Non-Elderly Americans Without Health Insurance, 2002-2003. p. 7 (Washington, DC: Families USA, 2004)

4 UNICEF, World Health Organization, United Nations Population Division and United Nations Statistics Division. Obtained from World Health Organization. Core Health Statistics. Accessed at http://www3.who.int/whosis/core/core_select_process.cfm?strISO3_select=CAN,FRA,DEU,ITA,JPN,GBR,USA&strIndicator_select=LEX0Male,LEX0Female,MortInfantBoth&intYear_select=latest&fixed=indicator&language=english on September 25, 2006

5 National Center for Health Statistics. CDC/NCHS, National Vital Statistics System, Mortality, Unpublished tables. Accessed at http://www.cdc.gov/nchs/data/statab/hist290_0039.pdf September 25, 2006.

6 UNICEF, World Health Organization, United Nations Population Division and United Nations Statistics Division. Obtained from World Health Organization. Core Health Statistics. Accessed at http://www3.who.int/whosis/core/core_select.cfm?path=whosis,core&language=english on September 25, 2006

7 Centers for Disease Control. "Achievements in Public Health, 1900-1999: Healthier Mothers and Babies," Accessed at http://www.cdc.gov/mmwr/preview/mmwrhtml/mm4838a2.htm on September 25, 2006

8 UNICEF. Age Specific Fertility Rate (15-19 years) 2000-2005. Accessed at http://www.childinfo.org/eddb/fertility/dbadol.htm on September 25, 2006

9 Child Health USA 2004. Vaccination Coverage. Accessed at http://www.mchb.hrsa.gov/mchirc/chusa_04/pages/0505vc.htm on September 25, 2006

10 Child Health USA 2004. Infant Mortality. Accessed at http://www.mchb.hrsa.gov/mchirc/chusa_04/pages/0406im.htm on September 25, 2006

11 Child Health USA 2004. International Infant Mortality Rates. Accessed at http://www.mchb.hrsa.gov/mchirc/chusa_04/pages/0405iimr.htm on September 25, 2006

12 Children's Defense Fund Action Council. "Stand Up For Children Now!" p. vi. (Washington, DC: Children's Defense Fund Action Council, 2006)

13 UNICEF, World Health Organization, United Nations Population Division and United Nations Statistics Division. Obtained from World Health Organization. Core Health Statistics. Accessed at http://www3.who.int/whosis/core/core_select.cfm?path=whosis,core&language=english on September 25, 2006

14 National Center for Health Statistics. "Health, United States, 2005: With Chartbook on Trends in the Health of Americans." Table 43, p. 214.

(Hyattsville, MD: National Center for Health Statistics, 2005)

15 Children's Defense Fund Action Council. "Stand Up For Children Now!"
p. vi. (Washington, DC: Children's Defense Fund Action Council, 2006)

16 UNICEF, World Health Organization, United Nations Population Division and United Nations Statistics Division. Obtained from World Organization. Core Health Statistics. Accessed at http://www3. who.int/whosis/core/core_select.cfm?path=whosis,core&language=en glish
on September 25, 2006

17 Centers for Disease Control and Prevention, National Center for Injury Prevention and Control. Web-based Injury Statistics Query and Reporting System (WISQARS) [online]. (2005) [cited Sept. 20, 2006]. Available from URL: www.cdc.gov/ncipc/wisqars

18 Child Welfare League of America. "Child Mental Health: Facts and Figures." Accessed at http://www.cwla.org/programs/bhd/mhfacts. htm#FACTSHEETS on September 25, 2006

19 Centers for Disease Control and Prevention. "Monitoring Developmental Disabilities." Accessed at http://www.cdc.gov/ncbddd/ dd/ddsurv.htm (and sub-pages for each type of disability) on September 25, 2006

20 Office of Applied Studies, Substance Abuse and Mental Health Services Administration, U.S. Department of Health & Human Services. "Children of Alcoholic and/or Substance Abusing Parents: Highlights." Accessed at http://www.oas.samhsa.gov/ACOA.htm on September 25, 2006

21 Parker, Emil and Jane Malone. "Administration Should Seek Increased Funding, Not Propose Drastic Cut In Key Lead Poisoning Prevention Program." P. 5 Accessed at http://campaign.childrensdefense.org/ childhealth/lead_poisoning.pdf on September 25, 2006

22 Organisation for Economic Co-operation and Development, Health Division. Government/social health insurance, Total health care, % of total population eligible, 2003. Accessed at http://www.sourceoecd. org/vl=610206/cl=26/nw=1/rpsv/ij/oecdstats/99991012/v1n1/s1/p1 on September 25, 2006.

23 Gladwell, Malcolm. "The Moral Hazard Myth." The New Yorker, August 29, 2005, p. 45.

24 Woolhandler, Steffie, Terry Campbell, and David U. Himmelstein. "Health Care Administration in the United States and Canada: Micromanagement, Macro Costs." International Journal of Health Services 34, no. 1 (2004): 65.

25 Anrig, Jr., Greg and Bernard Wasow. "Twelve Reasons Why Privatizing Social Security Is A Bad Idea," p. 12. (New York, NY: The Century Foundation, 2005)

26 Public Citizen and Physicians for a National Health Program. "Study Shows National Health Insurance Could Save $286 Billion on Health Care Paperwork: Authors say Medicare drug bill will increase bureaucratic costs, reward insurers and the AARP." (Washington, DC: Public Citizen,

January 14, 2004). Accessed at http://www.citizen.org/pressroom/print_ release.cfm?ID=1623 on September 25, 2006.

27 U.S. Census Bureau. "Statistical Abstract of the United States: 2006. Section 3: Health and Nutrition." (Washington, DC: U.S. Census Bureau, 2006).

28 The Center for Responsive Politics. Open Secrets Industry Totals: Health. Accessed at http://www.opensecrets.org/industries/indus. asp?ind=H&cycle=2006 on September 25, 2006.

29 America's Health Insurance Plans. Listed on home page at http:// www.ahip.org/. Accessed on September 25, 2006.

30 Woolhandler, Steffie, Terry Campbell, and David U. Himmelstein. "Health Care Administration in the United States and Canada: Micromanagement, Macro Costs." International Journal of Health Services 34, no. 1 (2004): 65.

31 The Center for Responsive Politics. Open Secrets Industry Totals: Health. Accessed at http://www.opensecrets.org/industries/indus. asp?ind=H&cycle=2006 on September 25, 2006.

32 Pear, Robert and Richard A. Oppel, Jr. "Results of Elections Give Pharmaceutical Industry New Influence in Congress." New York Times, November 21, 2002. Accessed at http://query.nytimes.com/gst/fullpage. html?sec=health&res=9402E1DB1439F932A15752C1A9649C8B63

33 Blendon, Robert J. et al., "Inequities in Health Care: A Five-Country Survey," Health Affairs, Vol. 21 No. 3, May/ June 2002

34 The Commonwealth Fund. "Medicare: Overview." Accessed at http://www. cmwf.org/topics/topics.htm?attrib_id=12013 on September 25, 2006

35 Weil, Alan J. "Can Medicaid Do More With Less?" (New York, NY: The Commonwealth Fund, 2006) Accessed at http://www.cmwf.org/publications/ publications_show.htm?doc_id=362793 on September 25, 2006.

36 Senator John Kerry. "Senator John Kerry "Kids First."" Press Release, January 27, 2005. Accessed at http://kerry.senate.gov/v3/cfm/record. cfm?id=231047& on September 25, 2006

37 Institute of Medicine. "Hidden Costs, Value Lost: Uninsurance in America." (Washington, DC: Institute of Medicine, 2003) Accessed at http://www. nap.edu/catalog/10719.html?onpi_newsdoc030908931X#description on September 25, 2006

38 Institute of Medicine. "Insuring America's Health: Principles and Recommendations." (Washington, DC: Institute of Medicine, 2004) Accessed at http://www.iom.edu/CMS/3809/4660/17632.aspx on September 25, 2006.

39 Mason-Dixon Polling and Research, 800 registered voters nationally conducted from July 5th to 10th, 2005.

40 George Bush, 2004 Republican Convention Acceptance Speech September 2, 2004

41 Broaddus, Matt. "Administration's Fiscal Year 2007 Budget is Likely Still to Leave SCHIP Coverage for Low-Income Children in Jeopardy." (Washington, DC: Center on Budget and Policy Priorities, 2006)

42 National Women's Law Center. "Women and Children Last—Again: An

Analysis of the President's FY 2007 Budget." (Washington, DC: National Women's Law Center, 2006)

43 National Women's Law Center. "Women and Children Last—Again: An Analysis of the President's FY 2007 Budget." (Washington, DC: National Women's Law Center, 2006)

44 National Women's Law Center. "Women and Children Last—Again: An Analysis of the President's FY 2007 Budget." (Washington, DC: National Women's Law Center, 2006)

45 Horney, James, Arloc Sherman, and Sharon Parrott. "Program Cuts in the President's Budget: Cuts Grow Deeper Over Time and Will Hit States Hard." (Washington, DC: Center on Budget and Policy Priorities, 2006)

46 National Women's Law Center. "Women and Children Last—Again: An Analysis of the President's FY 2007 Budget." (Washington, DC: National Women's Law Center, 2006)

47 Center on Budget and Policy Priorities. "The President's Budget: A Preliminary Analysis." (Washington, DC: Center on Budget and Policy Priorities, 2006)

48 Center on Budget and Policy Priorities. "The President's Budget: A Preliminary Analysis." (Washington, DC: Center on Budget and Policy Priorities, 2006)

49 Center on Budget and Policy Priorities. "The President's Budget: A Preliminary Analysis." (Washington, DC: Center on Budget and Policy Priorities, 2006)

50 DeNavas-Walt, Carmen, Bernadette D. Proctor, and Cheryl Hill Lee, U.S. Census Bureau, Current Population Reports, P60-231, Income, Poverty, and Health Insurance Coverage in the United States: 2005, Table C-1, p. 60, U.S. Government Printing Office, Washington, DC, 2006.

51 DeNavas-Walt, Carmen, Bernadette D. Proctor, and Cheryl Hill Lee, U.S. Census Bureau, Current Population Reports, P60-231, Income, Poverty, and Health Insurance Coverage in the United States: 2005, Table 10, p. 27, U.S. Government Printing Office, Washington, DC, 2006.

52 The Annie E. Casey Foundation, KIDS COUNT State Level Data Online, www.kidscount.org

53 The Annie E. Casey Foundation, KIDS COUNT State Level Data Online, www.kidscount.org

54 U.S. Census Bureau. Current Population Survey, 2006 Annual Social and Economic Supplement. Table HI05. Health Insurance Coverage Status and Type of Coverage by State and Age for All People: 2005. Accessed at http://pubdb3.census.gov/macro/032006/health/h05_000.htm on September 25, 2006.

55 DeNavas-Walt, Carmen, Bernadette D. Proctor, and Cheryl Hill Lee, U.S. Census Bureau, Current Population Reports, P60-231, Income, Poverty, and Health Insurance Coverage in the United States: 2005, Table 10, p. 27, U.S. Government Printing Office, Washington, DC, 2006.

56 The Annie E. Casey Foundation, KIDS COUNT State Level Data Online, www.kidscount.org

57 The Annie E. Casey Foundation, KIDS COUNT State Level Data Online, www.kidscount.org

58 The Annie E. Casey Foundation, KIDS COUNT State Level Data Online, www.kidscount.org

59 The Annie E. Casey Foundation, KIDS COUNT State Level Data Online, www.kidscount.org

60 The Annie E. Casey Foundation, KIDS COUNT State Level Data Online, www.kidscount.org

Chapter 3: *Child Abuse*
Citations

1 Urban Institute. "The Cost of Protecting Vulnerable Children V: Understanding State Variation in Child Welfare Financing." P. v (Washington, DC: Urban Institute, 2006)

2 Prevent Child Abuse America. "Total Estimated Cost of Child Abuse and Neglect In the United States: Statistical Evidence." (Chicago, IL: Prevent Child Abuse America, 2001)

3 U.S. Department of Health and Human Services, Administration on Children, Youth and Families. Child Maltreatment 2004 (Washington, DC: U.S. Government Printing Office, 2006).

4 U.S. Department of Health and Human Services, Administration on Children, Youth and Families. Child Maltreatment 2004 (Washington, DC: U.S. Government Printing Office, 2006).

5 Childhelp. "National Child Abuse Statistics." Accessed at http://www.childhelpusa.org/uploads/Gl/ci/GlciCz0RJ5B-BqEfR8Bh_w/STATS-2006.pdf on September 25, 2006.

6 Childhelp. "National Child Abuse Statistics." Accessed at http://www.childhelpusa.org/uploads/Gl/ci/GlciCz0RJ5B-BqEfR8Bh_w/STATS-2006.pdf on September 25, 2006.

7 Childhelp. "National Child Abuse Statistics." Accessed at http://www.childhelpusa.org/uploads/Gl/ci/GlciCz0RJ5B-BqEfR8Bh_w/STATS-2006.pdf on September 25, 2006.

8 American Academy of Pediatrics. "Health Topics: Sexual Abuse: What is child sexual abuse?" Accessed at http://www.aap.org/pubed/ZZZ1LW3YA7C.htm?&sub_cat=1 on September 25, 2006.

9 Childhelp. "National Child Abuse Statistics." Accessed at http://www.childhelpusa.org/uploads/Gl/ci/GlciCz0RJ5B-BqEfR8Bh_w/STATS-2006.pdf on September 25, 2006.

10 Child Welfare League of America. "National Fact Sheet 2006." Accessed at http://www.cwla.org/advocacy/nationalfactsheet06.htm on September 25, 2006.

11 Child Welfare League of America. National Data Analysis System.

http://ndas.cwla.org/

12 U.S. Department of Health and Human Services, Administration on Children, Youth and Families. Child and Family Service Reviews, Individual Key Findings Reports, 2001-2004. Accessed at http://basis.caliber.com/cwig/ws/cwmd/docs/cb_web/SearchForm on September 25, 2006.
13 Child Welfare League of America. National Data Analysis System. http://ndas.cwla.org/

14 NationMaster. "Child Maltreatment Deaths per 100,00 population under 15 (1990s)." Accessed at http://www.nationmaster.com/graph/hea_chi_mal_dea-health-child-maltreatment-deaths on September 25, 2006.

15 Child Welfare League of America. "Programs and Resources for Youth Aging Out of Foster Care." Accessed at http://cwla.org/programs/fostercare/agingoutresources.htm on September 25, 2006

16 Child Welfare League of America. "Youth After Foster Care." Accessed at http://www.cwla.org/programs/fostercare/factsheetafter.htm on September 25, 2006

17 Child Welfare League of America. "Youth After Foster Care." Accessed at http://www.cwla.org/programs/fostercare/factsheetafter.htm on September 25, 2006

18 Child Welfare League of America. "Youth After Foster Care." Accessed at http://www.cwla.org/programs/fostercare/factsheetafter.htm on September 25, 2006

19 U.S. Department of Health and Human Services, Office on Child Abuse and Neglect. "A Coordinated Response to Child Abuse and Neglect: The Foundation for Practice, Chapter Five: What Factors Contribute to Child Abuse and Neglect?" Accessed at http://www.childwelfare.gov/pubs/usermanuals/foundation/foundatione.cfm on September 25, 2006.

20 Child Welfare League of America. "Investing in the Future: Promoting the Well-Being of North Dakota's Children and Families." Washington, DC: Child Welfare League of America, 1994)

21 Prevent Child Abuse Georgia. "Cost of Child Abuse & Neglect in U.S. Estimated at $258 Million Per Day." Accessed at http://www.preventchildabusega.org/pdf/secure-charteredcouncil/Cost.of.child.abuse.pdf on October 31, 2006.

22 U.S. Department of Health and Human Services, Administration on Children, Youth and Families. Child Maltreatment 2004, Table 4-1, p.68. (Washington, DC: U.S. Government Printing Office, 2006).

23 Child Welfare League of America. National Data Analysis System. http://ndas.cwla.org/

24 U.S. Department of Commerce, Bureau of Economic Analysis. "National Income and Product Accounts Table: Table 2.4.5. Personal Consumption Expenditures by Type of Product." Accessed at http://www.bea.gov/bea/dn/nipaweb/TableView.asp?SelectedTable=69&FirstYear=2002&LastYear=2005&Freq=Year on October 6, 2006.

25 U.S. Department of Health and Human Services, Administration on Children, Youth and Families. Child Maltreatment 2004, Table 4-1, p. 68. (Washington, DC: U.S. Government Printing Office, 2006).

Chapter 4: *Prisons*

Citations

1 Justice Policy Institute. "The Punishing Decade: Prison and Jail Estimates at the Millennium." P.1 (Washington, DC: Justice Policy Institute, 2000)

2 Justice Policy Institute. "The Punishing Decade: Prison and Jail Estimates at the Millennium." P.3 (Washington, DC: Justice Policy Institute, 2000)

3 International Centre for Prison Studies. World Prison Brief. Accessed at http://www.prisonstudies.org/ on July 26, 2006

4 United Nations Office on Drugs and Crime, Division for Policy Analysis and Public Affairs. "United Nations Surveys of Crime Trends and Operations of Criminal Justice Systems, covering the period 1990 – 2002" Accessed at www.unodc.org/pdf/crime/eighthsurvey/8th_all_050331.xls on September 25, 2006; Japanese data from: Statistics Bureau & Statistical Research and Training Institute. "Historical Statistics of Japan: Chapter 28 Justice and Police." Accessed at http://www.stat.go.jp/english/data/chouki/index.htm; France data from: National Institute for Statistics and Economic Studies. Accessed at http://www.insee.fr/

5 World Health Organization. "World Report on Violence and Health." Table A.10, p. 322-323. (Geneva, Switzerland: World Health Organization, 2002)

6 The Sentencing Project. "Incarceration and Crime: A Complex Relationship." Figure 2, p. 2. (Washington, DC: The Sentencing Project, 2005)

7 Prison Policy Initiative. "The Prison Index: Taking the Pulse of the Crime Control Industry: Section II: Incarceration & Its Consequences." Accessed at http://www.prisonpolicy.org/prisonindex/penalcontrol.shtml on September 25, 2006.

8 Childhelp. "National Child Abuse Statistics." Accessed at http://www.childhelpusa.org/uploads/Gl/ci/GlciCz0RJ5B-BqEfR8Bh_w/STATS-2006.pdf on September 25, 2006.

9 Justice Policy Institute. "The Punishing Decade: Prison and Jail Estimates at the Millennium." P.5 (Washington, DC: Justice Policy Institute, 2000)

10 Justice Policy Institute. "The Punishing Decade: Prison and Jail Estimates at the Millennium." P.6 (Washington, DC: Justice Policy Institute, 2000)

11 Harrison, Paige M., & Allen J. Beck, Bureau of Justice Statistics, Prison and Jail Inmates at Midyear 2004 (Washington, DC: US Dept. of Justice, April 2005), p. 11

12 Harrison, Paige M., & Allen J. Beck, Bureau of Justice Statistics, Prison and Jail Inmates at Midyear 2004 (Washington, DC: US Dept. of Justice, April 2005), p. 11

13 The Eisenhower Foundation. "To Establish Justice, To Insure Domestic Tranquility." Accessed at http://www.eisenhowerfoundation.org/docs/justice.pdf on September 25, 2006.

14 The Eisenhower Foundation. "To Establish Justice, To Insure Domestic Tranquility." Accessed at http://www.eisenhowerfoundation.org/docs/justice.pdf on September 25, 2006.

15 Justice Policy Institute. "The Punishing Decade: Prison and Jail Estimates at the Millennium." P.5 (Washington, DC: Justice Policy Institute, 2000)

16 US Census Bureau "The Black Population in the United States: March 2002." P. 3. (Washington, DC: U.S. Census Bureau, 2003)

17 The Sentencing Project. "Incarceration and Crime: A Complex Relationship." p. 7. (Washington, DC: The Sentencing Project, 2005)

18 The Sentencing Project. "Factsheet: Women in Prison." (Washington, DC: The Sentencing Project, 2005)

19 The Sentencing Project. "Factsheet: Women in Prison." (Washington, DC: The Sentencing Project, 2005)

20 Prison Activist Resource Center. "Women in Prison." Accessed at http://prisonactivist.org/women/women-in-prison.html on September 25, 2006.

21 The Curry School of Education at the University of Virginia. "Women in Prison in the US: Facts and Figures." Accessed at http://curry.edschool.virginia.edu/index.php?option=com_content&task=view&id=728&Itemid=74 on September 25, 2006.

22 Mumola, Christopher J. "Incarcerated Parents and Their Children." P. 1-2 (Washington, DC: Bureau of Justice Statistics, 2000)

23 The Curry School of Education at the University of Virginia. "Women in Prison in the US: Facts and Figures." Accessed at http://curry.edschool.virginia.edu/index.php?option=com_content&task=view&id=728&Itemid=74 on September 25, 2006.

24 The Curry School of Education at the University of Virginia. "Women in Prison in the US: Facts and Figures." Accessed at http://curry.edschool.virginia.edu/index.php?option=com_content&task=view&id=728&Itemid=74 on September 25, 2006.

25 Mumola, Christopher J. "Incarcerated Parents and Their Children." P. 1-2 (Washington, DC: Bureau of Justice Statistics, 2000)

26 Mumola, Christopher J. "Incarcerated Parents and Their Children." P. 1-2 (Washington, DC: Bureau of Justice Statistics, 2000)

27 Mumola, Christopher J. "Incarcerated Parents and Their Children." P. 1-2 (Washington, DC: Bureau of Justice Statistics, 2000)

28 Child Welfare League of America. "Sacramento County community intervention program: Findings from a comprehensive study by community partners in child welfare, law enforcement, juvenile justice, and the Child Welfare League of America." (Washington, DC: Child Welfare League of America, 1997)

29 Child Welfare League of America. "Together Forward Leaving No Child Behind: Strengthening Mississippi's Child Welfare and Juvenile Justice Systems." (Washington, DC: Child Welfare League of America, 1992)

30 Ralph F. Boyd, Jr. Letter to Governor Ronnie Musgrove "Re: CRIPA Investigation of Oakley and Columbia Training Schools in Raymond and Columbia, Mississippi." Accessed at http://www.usdoj.gov/crt/split/documents/oak_colu_miss_findinglet.pdf on September 25, 2006.

31 Halbfinger, David M. "Care of Juvenile Offenders in Mississippi Is Faulted." New York Times, September 1, 2003

32 Juvenile Incarceration data from: Snyder, Howard N., and Sickmund, Melissa. "Juvenile Offenders and Victims: 2006 National Report." (Washington, DC: U.S. Department of Justice, Office of Justice Programs, Office of Juvenile Justice and Delinquency Prevention, 2006); Violent Crime Index from: Federal Bureau of Investigation. "Crime in the United States 2004: Uniform Crime Reports." (Washington, DC: Federal Bureau of Investigation, 2005)

33 Office of Juvenile Justice and Delinquency Prevention. "Juveniles in Corrections." (Washington, DC: U.S. Department of Justice, Office of Justice Programs, Office of Juvenile Justice and Delinquency Prevention, 2004)

34 Bureau of Justice Assistance. "Juveniles in Adult Prisons and Jails: A National Assessment" Accessed at http://www.ncjrs.gov/pdffiles1/bja/182503.pdf on September 25, 2006.

35 Coalition for Juvenile Justice. "Unlocking the Future: Detention Reform in the Juvenile Justice System." Accessed at http://www.juvjustice.org/publications/OverviewofAR03.pdf on September 25, 2006.

36 Coalition for Juvenile Justice. "Unlocking the Future: Detention Reform in the Juvenile Justice System." Accessed at http://www.juvjustice.org/publications/OverviewofAR03.pdf on September 25, 2006.

37 The Sentencing Project. "Critical Choices: New Options in Juvenile Crime Policy, 1999." (Washington, DC: The Sentencing Project, 1999)

38 Death Penalty Information Center. "Number of Executions by State and Region Since 1976." Accessed at http://www.deathpenaltyinfo.org/article.php?scid=8&did=186 on September 25, 2006.

39 Bureau of Justice Statistics. "Prisoners under State or Federal Jurisdiction." Accessed at http://www.ojp.usdoj.gov/bjs/data/corpop02.csv on September 25, 2006.

40 Bureau of Justice Statistics. "Prisoners under State or Federal Jurisdiction." Accessed at http://www.ojp.usdoj.gov/bjs/data/corpop02.csv on September 25, 2006. Rate calculated by dividing prison population numbers by U.S. Census Bureau. Adult Population data from 2004 American Community Survey.

41 Bureau of Justice Statistics. "Female prisoners under State or Federal jurisdiction." Accessed at http://www.ojp.usdoj.gov/bjs/data/corpop03.csv on September 25, 2006.

42 Federal Bureau of Investigation. "Crime in the United States 2004: Uniform Crime Reports." Table 4, p. 76-85. (Washington, DC: Federal Bureau of Investigation, 2005)

43 Federal Bureau of Investigation. "Crime in the United States 2004: Uniform Crime Reports." Table 4, p. 76-85. (Washington, DC: Federal Bureau of Investigation, 2005)

44 Bureau of Justice Statistics. "Prisoners under State or Federal jurisdiction." Accessed at http://www.ojp.usdoj.gov/bjs/data/corpop02.csv on September 25, 2006. Rate calculated by dividing prison population numbers by U.S. Census Bureau. Adult Population data from 2004 American Community Survey.

45 Snyder, Howard N., and Sickmund, Melissa. "Juvenile Offenders and Victims: 2006 National Report." (Washington, DC: U.S. Department of Justice, Office of Justice Programs, Office of Juvenile Justice and Delinquency Prevention, 2006)

Chapter 5: *Child Poverty*

Citations

1 U.S. Census Bureau. Data from the 2005 American Community Survey (Custom Data Tables). Accessed through http://factfinder.census.gov/servlet/DatasetMainPageServlet?_program=ACS&_submenuId=datasets_2&_lang=en on September 25, 2006.

2 National Center for Children in Poverty. "Who Are America's Poor Children?" Accessed at http://www.nccp.org/pub_cpt05b.html on September 25, 2006

3 US Department of Health and Human Services, Administration for Children and Families data accessed at http://www.acf.dhhs.gov/programs/ofa/caseload/2005/family05tanf.htm

4 National Center for Children in Poverty. "Basic Facts About Low-Income Children: Birth to Age 18." (New York, NY: National Center for Children in Poverty, 2005)

5 Burt, Martha R. "What Will it Take to End Homelessness?" (Washington, DC: Urban Institute, 2001).

6 National Low Income Housing Coalition. "Out of Reach 2005." (Washington, DC: National Low-Income Housing Coalition, 2005).

7 UNICEF. "Child Poverty in Rich Countries 2005." Innocenti Report Card No.6. Figure 9, p. 21 (Florence: UNICEF Innocent Research Centre, 2005).

8 DeNavas-Walt, Carmen, Bernadette D. Proctor, and Cheryl Hill Lee, U.S. Census Bureau, Current Population Reports, P60-231, Income, Poverty, and Health Insurance Coverage in the United States: 2005, Table B-2, p. 52, U.S. Government Printing Office, Washington, DC, 2006.

9 UNICEF. "Child Poverty in Rich Countries 2005." Innocenti Report Card No.6. Figure 9, p. 21 (Florence: UNICEF Innocent Research Centre, 2005).

10 DeNavas-Walt, Carmen, Bernadette D. Proctor, and Cheryl Hill Lee, U.S. Census Bureau, Current Population Reports, P60-231, Income, Poverty, and Health Insurance Coverage in the United States: 2005, Table B-2, p. 52, U.S. Government Printing Office, Washington, DC, 2006.

11 Leonhardt, David. "The Economics of Henry Ford May Be Pass_ in This Century." New York Times, April 5, 2006

12 Congressional Budget Office. Federal Spending on the Elderly and Children. Accessed at http://ftp.cbo.gov/showdoc.cfm?index=2300&sequence=0 on Sept. 20, 2006

13 DeNavas-Walt, Carmen, Bernadette D. Proctor, and Cheryl Hill Lee, U.S. Census Bureau, Current Population Reports, P60-231, Income, Poverty, and Health Insurance Coverage in the United States: 2005, U.S. Government Printing Office, Washington, DC, 2006. and National Center for Children in Poverty. "Basic Facts About Low-Income Children: Birth to Age 18." (New York, NY: National Center for Children in Poverty, 2005)

14 DeNavas-Walt, Carmen, Bernadette D. Proctor, and Cheryl Hill Lee, U.S. Census Bureau, Current Population Reports, P60-231, Income, Poverty, and Health Insurance Coverage in the United States: 2005, U.S. Government Printing Office, Washington, DC, 2006.

15 President Lyndon Johnson. "Annual Message to the Congress: The Economic Report of the President." (1964) Accessed at http://www.presidency.ucsb.edu/ws/index.php?pid=26004 on September 25, 2006.

16 DeNavas-Walt, Carmen, Bernadette D. Proctor, and Cheryl Hill Lee, U.S. Census Bureau, Current Population Reports, P60-231, Income, Poverty, and Health Insurance Coverage in the United States: 2005, Table B-2, p. 52, U.S. Government Printing Office, Washington, DC, 2006

17 Poverty data: DeNavas-Walt, Carmen, Bernadette D. Proctor, and Cheryl Hill Lee, U.S. Census Bureau, Current Population Reports, P60-231, Income, Poverty, and Health Insurance Coverage in the United States: 2005, Table B-2, p. 52, U.S. Government Printing Office, Washington, DC, 2006.; Dow Jones data: Accessed through a search at http://finance.yahoo.com/q/hp?s=%5EDJI Numbers represent value of the Dow Jones Industrial Average on the last day of the year. Accessed on September 20,2006

18 DeNavas-Walt, Carmen, Bernadette D. Proctor, and Cheryl Hill Lee, U.S. Census Bureau, Current Population Reports, P60-231, Income, Poverty, and Health Insurance Coverage in the United States: 2005, U.S. Government Printing Office, Washington, DC, 2006.

19 National Center for Children in Poverty. "Basic Facts About Low-Income Children: Birth to Age 18." (New York, NY: National Center for Children in Poverty, 2005)

20 Bureau of Labor Statistics. "Characteristics of Minimum Wage Workers: 2004." Accessed at http://www.bls.gov/cps/minwage2004tbls.htm on September 25, 2006

21 Bernstein, Jared and Isaac Shapiro. "Buying Power of Minimum Wage at 51-Year Low: Congress Could Break Record for Longest Period Without an Increase." Accessed at http://www.epinet.org/issuebriefs/224/ib224.pdf on September 25, 2006.

22 Minimum Wage figures calculated assuming a 52-week, 40-hour per week schedule at the federal minimum wage of $5.15 an hour; Congressional Salary data from: Dwyer, Paul E. "Salaries of Members of Congress: A List of Payable Rates and Effective Dates, 1789-2006." Accessed at http://www.senate.gov/reference/resources/pdf/97-1011.pdf#search=%22Congress%20salary%22 on September 25, 2006

23 Editorial. "Afflicting the Afflicted." New York Times, June 23, 2006.

24 Kennickell, Arthur B. "A Rolling Tide: Changes in the Distribution of Wealth in the U.S., 1989-2001," Table 10. (Annandale-on-Hudson, NY: Levy Economics Institute, 2003)

25 Office of Texas State Senator Eliot Shapleigh. "Texas on the Brink: How Texas Ranks Among the 50 States." Rankings updated where appropriate.

Accessed at http://www.bayareanewdemocrats.org/files/texasrankings.pdf #search=%22%22Texas%20on%20the%20Brink%22%22 on September 25, 2006.

26 National Women's Law Center. "Women and Children Last—Again: An Analysis of the President's FY 2007 Budget." (Washington, DC: National Women's Law Center, 2006)

27 National Women's Law Center. "Women and Children Last—Again: An Analysis of the President's FY 2007 Budget." (Washington, DC: National Women's Law Center, 2006)

28 Horney, James, Arloc Sherman, and Sharon Parrott. "Program Cuts in the President's Budget: Cuts Grow Deeper Over Time and Will Hit States Hard." (Washington, DC: Center on Budget and Policy Priorities, 2006)

29 National Coalition for the Homeless. "Bush Budget Leaves No Millionaire Behind as he Proposes Massive Cuts to Programs for Homeless and Low-Income People." Accessed at http://www.nationalhomeless.org/housing/budgetfeb14.html on September 12, 2006.

30 The Annie E. Casey Foundation, KIDS COUNT State Level Data Online, www.kidscount.org

31 Nord, Mark, Margaret Andrews and Steven Carlson. "Household Food Security in the United States, 2004." (Washington, DC: United States Department of Agriculture, 2005).

32 National Center for Children in Poverty. 50-State Policy Data Wizard. Accessed at http://www.nccp.org/wizard/wizard.cgi?action=X&page=pol_1 on August 30, 2006

33 The Annie E. Casey Foundation, KIDS COUNT State Level Data Online, www.kidscount.org

34 National Center for Children in Poverty. 50-State Policy Data Wizard. Accessed at http://www.nccp.org/wizard/wizard.cgi?action=X&page=pol_1 on August 30, 2006

35 The Annie E. Casey Foundation, KIDS COUNT State Level Data Online, www.kidscount.org

36 Children's Defense Fund. "State of America's Children 2005." Table B1-1, p. 173. (Washington, DC: Children's Defense Fund, 2006)

Chapter 6: *Taxes and Government*

Citations

1 Brown, Dorothy A. "A Tax Credit or a Handout?" New York Times, April 18, 2006.

2 Grover Norquist, on NPR's Morning Edition, May 25, 2001.

3 Sagoo, Sumeet. "Federal Tax Burdens and Expenditures by State: Which States Gain Most from Federal Fiscal Operations?" Figure 1, p. 1. (Washington, DC: Tax Foundation, 2004)

4 U.S. Census Bureau. Current Population Survey, 2006 Annual Social and Economic Supplement. Table HI05. Health Insurance Coverage Status and Type of Coverage by State and Age for All People: 2005. Accessed at http://pubdb3.census.gov/macro/032006/health/h05_000.htm on September 25, 2006.

5 Families USA. "Medicaid: Good Medicine for State Economies 2004 Update." P.8 (Washington, DC: Families USA, 2004).

6 Broaddus, Matt. "Administration's Fiscal Year 2007 Budget is Likely Still to Leave SCHIP Coverage for Low-Income Children in Jeopardy." (Washington, DC: Center on Budget and Policy Priorities, 2006)

7 Scarcella, Cynthia Andrews, Roseana Bess, Erica Hecht Zielewski, and Rob Geen. "The Cost of Protecting Vulnerable Children V: Understanding State Variation in Child Welfare Financing." (Washington, DC: Urban Institute, 2006)

8 Schulman, Karen and Helen Blank. "Child Care Assistance Policies 2005: States Fail to Make Up Lost Ground, Families Continue to Lack Critical Supports." (Washington, DC: National Women's Law Center, 2005)

9 U.S. Department of Health and Human Services, Administration on Children, Youth and Families. "Head Start Program Fact Sheet, FY 2004." Accessed at http://www.acf.hhs.gov/programs/hsb/research/2005.htm on September 19, 2006.

10 Food Research and Action Center. "State of the States: 2005." (Washington, DC: Food Research and Action Center, 2005)

11 United States Department of Agriculture. "WIC Program Participation And Costs." Accessed at http://www.fns.usda.gov/pd/wisummary.htm on September 11, 2006.

12 United States Department of Agriculture. "Food Stamp Program Participation and Costs." Accessed at http://www.fns.usda.gov/pd/fssummar.htm on September 11, 2006.

13 House Ways and Means Committee Green Book, WMCP: 108-6, 2004 Green Book, Section 13

14 Greenstein, Robert. "The Earned Income Tax Credit: Boosting Employment, Aiding The Working Poor." (Washington, DC: Center on Budget and Policy Priorities, 2005)

15 Mason-Dixon Polling and Research, 800 registered voters nationally conducted from February 19th to 27th, 2003.

16 Mason-Dixon Polling and Research, 800 registered voters nationally conducted from February 19th to 27th, 2003.

17 William G. Gale and Peter R. Orszag. "Sunsets In The Tax Code." (Washington, DC: Brookings Tax Policy Center, 2003)

18 Friedman, Joel. "Overview Of Final Budget Resolution Agreement Large Tax Cuts In Budget Would Worsen Long-Term Fiscal Outlook." (Washington, DC: Center on Budget and Policy Priorities, 2003)

19 High Scope/Perry Preschool research results: Schweinhart, L.J., Barnes, H.V., & Weikart, D.P. (1993). Significant benefits: The High/Scope Perry Preschool study through age 27. Ypsilanti, MI: High/Scope Press.Dr. Barnett on High

Scope/Perry Preschool cost savings: Barnett, S.W. (1993).

20 Taggart, R. (1998). The Quantum Opportunities Program. In D. S. Elliott (Series Ed.), Blueprints for violence prevention: Bookfour. Boulder, CO: Center for the Study and Prevention of Violence.RAND Corporation on cost analysis of Quantum Opportunities:Greenwood, P.W. et al. (1996).

21 Diverting children from a life of crime: Measuring costs and benefits. Santa Monica, CA: RAND. Dr. Cohen on savings of preventing youth crime: Cohen, M. A. (1997).

22 Prevent Child Abuse America. "Total Estimated Cost of Child Abuse and Neglect In the United States: Statistical Evidence." (Chicago, IL: Prevent Child Abuse America, 2001)

23 U.S. Office of Management and Budget. "Budget of the United States Government, Fiscal Year 2007: Historical Tables." Table 1.1, p. 22. Accessed at http://www.whitehouse.gov/omb/budget/fy2007/pdf/hist.pdf on September 25, 2006.

24 Bernasek, Anna "'Temporary' Tax Cuts Have a Way of Becoming Permanent." New York Times, May 14, 2006.

25 Office of Tax Analysis, U.S. Department of the Treasury. "A Dynamic Analysis of Permanent Extension of the President's Tax Relief." (Washington, DC: U.S. Department of the Treasury, 2006)

26 Urbina, Ian. "With Parents Absent, Trying to Keep Child Care in the Family." New York Times, July 23, 2006.

27 Johnston, David Cay. "I.R.S. Will Cut Tax Lawyers Who Audit the Richest." New York Times, July 23, 2006.

28 Michelle Singletary "Book offers cautionary tale for parents." Washington Post, July 9, 2006.

29 Shapiro, Isaac and Joel Friedman. "New CBO Data Indicate Growth in Long Term Income Inequality Continues." (Washington, DC: Center on Budget and Policy Priorities, 2006)

30 Shailagh Murray "In Congress, a Budget Divide" Washington Post, May 18, 2006

31 U.S. Department of the Treasury. "The 2006 Annual Report Of The Board Of Trustees Of The Federal Old-Age And Survivors Insurance And Federal Disability Insurance Trust Funds" Accessed at http://www.treasury.gov/offices/economic-policy/reports/oasdi.pdf on September 19, 2006.

32 Internal Revenue Service. Data accessed at www.irs.gov/pub/irs-soi/03in05tr.xls on August 15, 2006.

33 Citizens for Tax Justice. "99% of Americans Are Net Losers Under Bush Tax and Spending Policies." (Washington, DC: Citizens for Tax Justice, 2006).

34 Citizens for Tax Justice. "99% of Americans Are Net Losers Under Bush Tax and Spending Policies." (Washington, DC: Citizens for Tax Justice, 2006).

35 Tax Foundation. "History of the Income Tax in the United States." Accessed at http://www.infoplease.com/ipa/A0005921.html on September 26, 2006.

36 U.S. Census Bureau, Governments Division. "States Ranked by Total Taxes and Per Capita Amount: 2004." Accessed at http://www.census.gov/govs/statetax/04staxrank.html on September 7, 2006.

37 U.S. Census Bureau, Governments Division. "States Ranked by Revenue and Expenditure Total Amount and Per Capita Total Amount: 2004" Accessed at http://ftp2.census.gov/govs/state/04rank.pdf on September 7, 2006.

38 NationMaster. "The percentage of gross earnings given up in tax, including any social security contributions. Calculated for a married couple with two children, earning 100% of the average wage. Data for 2001." Accessed at http://www.nationmaster.com/graph/tax_tot_tax_wed_sin_inc_fam-tax-wedge-single-income-family on September 1, 2006

39 NationMaster. "Total taxation as % of GDP by country." Accessed at http://www.nationmaster.com/graph/tax_tot_tax_as_of_gdp-taxation-total-as-of-gdp on September 25, 2006.

40 Tax Foundation. "Total Income by State, Per Capita, 2005." Downloaded from http://www.taxfoundation.org/files/ffhandbook-20060309.xls on June 6, 2006. and "State and Local Tax Burdens by State, 1970-2005." Downloaded from http://www.taxfoundation.org/files/f948a1caa4814862c726fa5e4c64c554.xls on June 6, 2006.

41 Tax Foundation. "State and Local Tax Burdens by State, 1970-2005." Downloaded from http://www.taxfoundation.org/files/f948a1caa4814862c726fa5e4c64c554.xls on June 6, 2006. and The Annie E. Casey Foundation, KIDS COUNT State Level Data Online, www.kidscount.org

Michael R. Petit

President and Founder
Every Child Matters Education Fund

Michael Petit founded the Every Child Matters Education Fund in 2002 with the mission of making children's issues a political priority.

Mr. Petit served as deputy director at the Child Welfare League of America and as Maine's commissioner of human services. He has consulted extensively across the U.S. on a wide variety of children's issues. Mr. Petit also was a delegate to the United Nations Convention on the Rights of the Child in Helsinki, Finland.

He is a Maine native with three grown daughters and four grandchildren. He holds a Bachelors degree from Bowdoin College and a Masters in Social Work from Boston College.

book@everychildmatters.org